WRITTEN BY
Andy Chambers, Pete Haines,
Andy Hoare, Phil Kelly
& Graham McNeill

ADDITIONAL TEXT BY
Steve Cumiskey

INTERNAL ART
Alex Boyd, Paul Dainton, Des Hanley,
Nuala Kennedy, Karl Kopinski,
Adrian Smith & John Wigley

COVER ART
Karl Kopinski

GRAPHIC DESIGN
Stefan Kopinski

MINIATURES DESIGNERS
Tim Adcock, Juan Diaz, Jes Goodwin,
Mark Harrison, Brian Nelson,
Alan Perry, Michael Perry.

MODELS & SCENERY
Mark Jones & Kirsten Williams

PRODUCTION & LAYOUT
John Michelbach, Mark Owen
& Nathan Winter

MINIATURES PAINTERS
Kev Asprey, Neil Green, Tammy Haye,
Darren Latham, Neil Langdown,
Seb Perbet, Keith Robertson
& Kirsten Williams

Special thanks to the
Ancient and Honourable
Order of Tech Priests

Excerpt from the novel "First & Only" by Dan Abnett and Gaunt's Ghosts artwork courtesy the Black Library.

UK
Games Workshop Ltd.,
Willow Rd, Lenton,
Nottingham,
NG7 2WS

US
Games Workshop Inc.,
6721 Baymeadow Drive,
Glen Burnie,
Maryland 21060-6401

Canada
2679 Bristol Circle,
Units 2&3,
Oakville,
Ontario, L6H 6Z8

Australia
Games Workshop,
23 Liverpool Street,
Ingleburn
NSW 2565

Japan
Games Workshop Ltd.,
Willow Rd, Lenton,
Nottingham,
NG7 2WS

V: 1-84154-410-8   Games Workshop Web site: http://www.games-workshop.com   Product code: 60 03 01 05 003

CODEX: IMPERIAL GUARD

"Listen and remember. You are Imperial Guardsmen now. It does not matter to me whether you come from Catachan or Valhalla. I don't care whether you are a volunteer or were rounded up by an enlistment gang. I will teach you to march like Imperial Guardsmen. I will teach you to maintain and fire your lasguns like Imperial Guardsmen. I will teach you to fight like Imperial Guardsmen and that means learning every dirty trick in the segmentum. Most importantly, I will teach you your duty and you will do it without hesitation, on command. The reason you will do this is because our immortal Lord, the Emperor of Mankind, owns your pitiful lives, and if there is one worthwhile thing you will ever do it is to honour your debt to Him."

The Imperial Guard is the largest and most diverse organisation the galaxy has ever seen. It contains billions of men from a million different worlds. Half-feral savages march alongside former hive plant workers. Men whose home was blistering desert, tropical jungle, icy steppe or desolate moorland are united under the banner of the Imperium of Man. The entire diversity of the massive Imperium is encapsulated in its ranks.

The power of the Imperial Guard does not lie in numbers alone. It is equipped with lumbering but deadly battle tanks, fast-striding walkers and the heaviest artillery known. Whole worlds are dedicated to the production of the war machines of the Imperial Guard which, while inelegant, are fearsomely practical.

Despite its awesome power, however, the Imperial Guard constantly struggles to protect the Imperium from its many enemies. The mighty Tyranid hive fleets batter at the Eastern Fringe, Ork Waaaghs erupt without warning or pause, the damned Traitor Legions pour from the Eye of Terror hungry for Mankind's souls, mysterious Eldar raiders strike without mercy, the ancient Necrons sally from their tomb worlds and numerous emergent empires, such as the Tau, rise up to challenge Humanity's mastery. Against these diverse and often incomprehensible threats, the Imperial Guard pits human resolve and ingenuity in an unending battle with an inimical universe.

> In any army, balance is the key to success. A commander who puts his faith in heavy weaponry alone will be outmanoeuvred. A commander who relies on close combat without support will lose his force to enemy fire. Each element must work in harmony, so that the effectiveness of the army is greater than the sum of its parts.
>
> The Tactica Imperium

WHY COLLECT AN IMPERIAL GUARD ARMY?

In the midst of genetically engineered super-beings, alien killing machines, warrior mystics, and technology that approaches sorcery in its sophistication, the Imperial Guard are mere soldiers. Clad in a flak jacket and carrying a lasgun, they have to contend with the most terrifying threats, relying on numbers, massed firepower and a bayonet with some guts behind it. As such it is easy to identify with these brave souls and to see in them the qualities of true heroes.

If the humanity of the Imperial Guard does not appeal, there is every chance that their vast range of armoured fighting vehicles will. From the fast-moving Sentinel to the heavy Leman Russ, the Imperial Guard has an excellent choice of armour with which to wage war. While the infantry of the Imperial Guard is its anvil, the tanks are its hammer, and with the right coordination of the two arms there is no enemy that can't be battered into submission.

Of all the armies in Warhammer 40,000, the Imperial Guard has the potential to field the most models. This needn't be the case, but if an impressively large army is what you are looking for then you need look no further than the Imperial Guard. Even with a generous amount of vehicles, an Imperial Guard army can field upwards of a hundred men in a standard 1,500 points game, and the sight of so many figures arrayed in close order firing lines beneath their standards is an awesome sight.

Finally, the Imperial Guard presents enormous opportunities to an experienced modeller. There are hundreds of different regiments and, although Games Workshop produces the miniatures to do many of them, by combining different plastic sets and converting existing models it is possible to field a regiment that is uniquely yours. The doctrine rules in this book enable you to personalise your forces even more, so that your Imperial Guard army is indelibly stamped with your own personality.

Gaunt leapt to his feet, knocking the camp table over. It was the sudden motion rather than the scream of incoming shells which made Caffran leap up in shock. Gaunt was scrabbling for his side-arm, hanging in its holster on a hook by the steps. He grabbed the speech-horn of the vox-caster set, slung under the racks that held his books.

'Gaunt to all units! To arms! To arms! Prepare for maximum resistance!'

Caffran didn't wait for any further instruction. He was already up the steps and banging through the gas curtains as volleys of shells assaulted their trenches. Huge plumes of vaporised mud spat up from the trench head behind him and the narrow gully was full of yells of suddenly animated guardsmen. A shell whinnied down low across his position and dug a hole the size of a drop-ship behind the rear breastwork of the trench. Liquid mud drizzled down on him. Caffran pulled his lasgun from its sling and slithered up towards the top of the trench firestep. There was chaos, panic, troopers hurrying every direction, screaming and shouting.

Was this it? Was this the final moment in the long, drawn-out conflict they had found themselves in? Caffran tried to slide up the side of the trench far enough to get a sight over the lip, across no man's land to the enemies' emplacements which they had been locked into for the last six months. All he could see was a mist of smoke and mud.

There was a crackle of las weapons and several screams. More shells fell. One of them found the centre of a nearby communications trench. Then the screaming became real and immediate. The drizzle that fell on him was no longer water and mud. There were body parts in it.

Caffran cursed and wiped the sight-lens of his lasgun clean of filth. Behind him he heard a shout, a powerful voice that echoed along the traverses of the trench and seemed to shake the duckboards. He looked back to see Commissar Gaunt emerging from his dugout.

Gaunt was dressed now in his full dress uniform and cap, the camo-cloak of his adopted regiment swirling about his shoulder, his face a mask of bellowing rage. In one hand he held his bolt pistol and in the other his chainsword, which whined and sang in the early morning air.

'In the name of Tanith! Now they are on us we must fight! Hold the line and hold your fire until they come over the mud wall!'

Caffran felt a rejoicing in his soul. The commissar was with them and they would succeed, no matter the odds. Then something closed down his world with a vibratory shock that blew mud up into the air and seemed to separate his spirit from his body.

The section of trench had taken a direct hit. Dozens of men were dead. Caffran lay stunned in a broken line of duckboard and splattered mud. A hand grabbed him by the shoulder and hauled him up. Blinking he looked up to see the face of Gaunt. Gaunt looked at him with a solemn, yet inspiring gaze.

'Sleeping after a good breakfast?' the commissar enquired of the bewildered trooper.

'No sir... I ... I...'

The crack of lasguns and needle lasers began to whip around them from the armoured loopholes on the trench head. Gaunt wrenched Caffran back to his feet.

'I think the time has come,' Gaunt said 'and I'd like all of my brave men in the line with me when we advance.'

Spitting out grey mud, Caffran laughed. 'I'm with you, sir,' he said, 'from Tanith to wherever we end up.'

Caffran heard the whine of Gaunt's chainsword as the commissar leapt up the scaling ladder nailed to the trench wall above the firestep and yelled to his men.

'Men of Tanith! Do you want to live forever?'

Their reply, loud and raucous, was lost in the barrage of shells. But Ibram Gaunt knew what they had said.

Weapons blazing, Gaunt's Ghosts went over the top and blasted their way towards glory, death or whatever else awaited them in the smoke.

from First & Only by Dan Abnett

ORIGINS AND HISTORY OF THE IMPERIAL GUARD

The vast organisation known as the Imperial Guard has been the backbone of the Imperium's fighting forces for uncounted centuries. Its earliest origins can be traced back to the so-called 'Imperial Army' of the Great Crusades at the dawn of the age of the Imperium. At some point, either prior to, or more likely during the cataclysmic events of the Horus Heresy, the army became known as the Imperial Guard. As with so much of the earliest histories of the Imperium, this transition can only be glimpsed through a limited number of sources which have survived the tide of millennia in crumbling reliquaries and data-stacks.

Unfortunately, these are often complicated by commentaries and postulations of later periods after much knowledge was suppressed or lost. For example, in the dusty pict-archives of Enfield IV, obscure but extensive records can be found on the 13th/5th Imperial Army formation of 'Hylgar's Hellraisers'. These are listed as a contemporary unit of the 41st millennium (circa 975-988.M41) but this is patently a later copy from an earlier reference. The formation is listed in no contemporary order of battle – not in itself unusual but for the fact that the formation's leader, Julius Hylgar, is listed as bearing the titles Cardinal of Kolarne, Imperial Commander and holder of the Grand Marnier Militaris (curiously, no other reference has ever been found to this title). No individual has been permitted both Ecclesiarchical and military ranks since the terrible events of Vandire's Reign of Blood and the Age of Apostasy in the 36th millennium.

Furthermore, the units of the formation exhibit a frankly puzzling assortment of weapons and troops, including mutants and grav-vehicles. All such units were outlawed after the Horus Heresy according to the earliest volumes of the Tactica Imperium. Therefore it is eminently likely that the 13th/5th date back to before this time, probably to the early 31st millennium.

No conclusive information can be gained from further investigation however. As with so much of the origins of the Imperial Guard, knowledge can only be pieced together through speculation and supposition based around known events, as Hylgar's Hellraisers amply demonstrate.

THE GREAT CRUSADES
It is known that the Emperor began the crusades from Earth, his silver fleets carrying forth legions of genetically enhanced Space Marine warriors to liberate Humanity from the clutches of aliens, the dark paths of ignorance and the malign influence of the Chaos gods. The crushing victories and occasional defeats of the Emperor's legions are the stuff of legend but it is clear that, wherever possible, the Emperor and most of his Primarchs attempted to win over control of Human populations and incorporate them into the fight to liberate ever more worlds.

Do not strike until you are ready to crush the enemy utterly, and then attack without mercy, destroy every vestige of resistance, leave no one to work against you.

The Tactica Imperium

This then would be the earliest instance of the Imperial army, a doubtless dizzying profusion of men drawn from different worlds: adventurers, mercenaries, idealists, undesirables, xenophobes, primitives and opportunists. At first these would have been employed almost exclusively for garrison duty on their own worlds. With the acknowledged support of the Emperor, these effectively loyalist local forces kept rebellions in check and defended against alien raiders.

Again, hard evidence of such is difficult to find. Faded holo-images from the once-famed crystal gallery in the lost citadel of the Kromarch on El'Phanor show a triptych from the Great Crusade where Human troops can be clearly identified fighting alongside the Luna Wolves Space Marine Legion; troops in what appears to be archaic mesh armour and wielding rifles of unidentifiable type can be seen participating in the liberation of an unknown world, possibly El'Phanor itself.

However, as the relentless mathematics of building a galactic empire pushed the Space Marine legions further apart, these loyalists started being moved off-world. First they would most likely be employed for garrison duty and mopping up on worlds in the wake of the legions. Eventually, certainly by the time the legions approached the Eastern Fringe, the Imperial Army would have been deployed at the forefront of the crusades.

A good general does not lead an army to destruction just because he knows it will follow.

The Tactica Imperium

This ties in with one of the tenets of Imperial Guard organisation in later millennia, that of regimental formation. Many sources concur that the basis for regimental formations is what would fit into the interstellar ships available to the crusades – typically producing three thousand man regiments which can be carried by a single transport vessel or one of the many available classes of cruiser. In the crusades, army and fleet functioned as a single entity, with army commanders exercising overall command of both elements. Regiments were commonly assigned to a specific vessel, and deployment of that ship intrinsically brought a large body of fighting men with it who could undertake landings and garrison duties as required.

This approach ensured that an individual regiment was deployed with each ship. It was doubtless a brutal but necessary equation; the losses of ships in the Warp or through enemy action did not result in remnants being left scattered among other vessels. Naturally the importance of keeping men from individual worlds together to form the natural bond of brothers in arms was also an important element in creating cohesive fighting formations. In many cases, men from different worlds could barely understand each other's languages, let alone the nuances of social mores and customs, tactics or special equipment which influence a formation's efficiency in combat. All of these elements laid the groundwork for the traditions still seen today – that a regiment is recruited from a single world and stays together and fights together wherever possible.

Carnage at Fortress Carcasson: The 9th Cadian devastates Hive Fleet Scarabus

However, over the course of campaigns, regiments are invariably whittled down by casualties, necessitating the combination of shattered formations into ad hoc groupings. References exist in Codicium Arkathalor (a fragmentary record of the campaigns of the Pandora sector in the late 30th millennium) to 'split' regimental formations such as the 17th/21st Tiger Lizards and the 61st/320th Orenian. The codex makes it clear these were mixed formations made up of heavily mauled regiments combined to return them to being effective fighting formations.

Likewise, some specialised troops, such as xeno-cavalry or Ogryns, have apparently always been split between larger formations to bolster their efforts. Their specialised capabilities make them unwieldy to operate at regimental scale, except in certain rare and often excessively emphasised campaigns. The ancient traditions of splitting specialised regiments and recombining remnants are the subject of heated debate between Imperial commanders to this day.

Many commanders declare that the reduced efficiency of combined regiments makes them barely worth their rations; infighting and mistrust make the diverse elements function as less than the sum of their parts and mutinies are commonplace. Others are interested only in the number of men at arms that can be fielded – their successful integration as fighting units is of less interest than their physical size. The Tactica Imperium presents both viewpoints as equally valid.

The first Imperial commissars emerged as a tool for ensuring proper integration of remnant regiments, and by the 31st millennium their role expanded to maintaining the quality and morale of all Imperial regiments. At the onset of the Horus Heresy, the first rebellious act of traitor units was to kill their commissars, while in loyalist regiments commissars were often forced to take extreme measures to maintain discipline, earning them their reputation for steadfastness and calculated brutality.

It also appears that, initially, it was common practice for regiments to be subordinated to the Space Marine legions in some regions, whereas in others overall command rested with the Imperial governor. By the onset of the Horus Heresy it became very apparent what a mistake it had been to place army units under Space Marine control. Among the traitors, almost all formations uniformly followed their masters into rebellion, out of fear or blind faith. Even amongst the loyalists, Imperial units with an officer cadre of enhanced warriors performed poorly, usually driven to destruction by the inability of the unaugmented humans to keep up with the demands of their indefatigable Space Marine leaders.

Over the course of the Heresy, entire armies were raised and squandered both by the Great Enemy and the desperate loyalist commanders. From the gigantic tank battles of Tallarn to the bloodbath of trench warfare on Omicron Epsilon, the Imperial army tore itself apart. Combined forces of fleet and army elements moved from world to world at the command of generals and lord commanders whose loyalties were unknown to both sides. Thousands of small empires were carved out by ambitious commanders with no true loyalty to either side. Over the course of following centuries, and at a cost of billions of lives, the Imperium was reforged, forever tainted by the blood spilt in the massive civil war which almost destroyed it.

In the aftermath of the Heresy, massive changes were made to the Imperial army. By this time, it was undoubtedly known universally as the Imperial Guard. The link between fleet and army was severed – never again were Imperial Guard commanders given direct control over interstellar ships. Centrally trained commissars were universally introduced to watch for disloyalty and recidivism on the part of newly-recruited officers and their regiments.

Almost without exception this has limited the ability of the Imperial Guard to mutiny en masse in subsequent millennia; only during the Age of Apostasy have whole armies and sectors betrayed their oaths of loyalty to the Emperor. In those turbulent times, few could be sure of just which commanders truly followed the directives of Him on Earth, and who pursued their own overweening ambitions. With the curbs on the might of the Ecclesiarchy which followed, the Imperial Guard has achieved its current status; a byword for loyalty and honour which, with a few notable exceptions, is well-deserved.

THE TACTICA IMPERIUM

The Tactica Imperium is the most widespread manual employed by the Imperial Guard. It is not a single tome, however, and has no one author; instead it is a whole collection of documents, doctrines, manuals and notes approved for inclusion by the Departmento Munitorum and the office of the Lord Commander Militant of the Imperial Guard. The collection of books comprising the Tactica is therefore constantly being updated, often at a different pace, as the sheer size of the Imperium precludes any true standardisation.

The Tactica's origins lie in the days of the Emperor's Great Crusade. In those times, vast forces were being raised quickly and it was apparent some standardisation was needed to make them function as a whole. Any available texts were seized on and distributed to provide at least some guidance. Over time this initial collection expanded.

Now contained within the Tactica are treatises on construction of field fortifications, the correct evolutions of close order drill, the oaths of allegiance to be made by new recruits and the statutes of military law. Many of these are adopted verbatim, although some are best viewed metaphorically. The tactical treatises in particular are subject to many different interpretations. Their value lies in provoking thought and, through it, understanding of the core principles so these can then be applied by a good commander as needed.

The Tactica cannot be taken too literally though. In war, circumstances change too quickly to refer every decision to a book. Its virtue is that it provides a reference for new officers and there is always a chance that guidance can be found on a critical issue.

ORGANISATION OF THE IMPERIAL GUARD

Across the million worlds that constitute the Imperium of Man, the primary defence against any alien or heretical threat is the Imperial Guard. There are more specialised organisations; the Inquisitorial Ordos stand ready to oppose the direst threats. There are organisations with more firepower; the Titan Legions of the Adeptus Mechanicus and the war fleets of the Imperial Navy can lay waste to entire cities in a matter of hours. There are more elite troops; the genetically engineered warriors of the Adeptus Astartes stand at the pinnacle of human capability – indeed, some would even say they have transcended Humanity. Despite this, none can doubt that the Imperial Guard is the most vital element of Humanity's defence.

From the ice halls of Valhalla to the steaming jungles of Catachan, from the perpetual night of Mordia to the blistering deserts of Tallarn, uncounted millions of soldiers stand ready to crush the Emperor's enemies. They are, by and large, normal men but are often the product of warrior cultures that reach back over the millennia, all firmly rooted in the martial pride of Terra. Within the Imperium, the sheer diversity of ancient cultures breeds countless types of soldier but within the Imperial Guard this diversity is controlled and shaped to fashion an almost unstoppable weapon of war. Given the sheer size of the Imperium, this is a remarkable testament to the organisation of the Imperial war machine.

The Imperium is so vast that central control of its widespread domains is practically impossible. Often it is difficult enough to ensure that far-flung worlds remain loyal to the Emperor's cause, so controlling the day-to-day activities of these planets is a hopeless task. Because of this, the building blocks of the Imperial Guard are firmly based on the military forces of individual worlds. Some Imperial worlds are governed by the Ministorum, the church of the Divine Emperor, while others are controlled by the Adeptus Mechanicus. There are even some garrison worlds administered as military societies by the Imperial Guard itself. These are in a minority however. The majority of worlds are independently governed by Imperial commanders, normally with the approval and support of the Adeptus Terra, although events sometimes move faster than the distant bureaucracy can keep up with. Imperial commanders, also known as planetary governors, are the scions of powerful noble families, each with their own power base and the means to maintain control without any routine support from the Imperium.

Each Imperial commander is responsible for defending his own world. This is essential – warp communication is unreliable as is warp travel. Without local defences, an enemy could overwhelm a world before any forces could be despatched to its aid, even were such aid available. Local forces are generally categorised as planetary defence forces, they are intended to be fully capable of defending their world against most attacks and to be able to keep even a powerful enemy at bay long enough for Imperial support to be despatched. The promise of Imperial support and the right to rule a world in the name of the Immortal Emperor comes at a price however. Each commander is a sworn vassal of the Emperor and is responsible for providing military service in return. In the early days of the Imperium, this military service was a straightforward pledge to bring a set number of followers and fight in person. This approach was shown to be too inflexible as the Imperium grew and was replaced with a tithe. The tithe is assessed according to the wealth and resources of the world and can be taken in the form of men or materiel. The method of assessment is arcane to say the least, and taxes the abilities of countless adepts and scribes. When a tithe is taken as troops, soldiers will be recruited in much the same way as the planetary defence force is recruited. Sometimes, the regiments raised are identical, the tithe being drawn from the PDF. On other occasions, the regiments needed are raised specifically for service in the Imperial Guard. Normally, a tithe will be in two parts, the first being a regular obligation that is supplied regardless of circumstances, the second being an obligation that can be demanded in response to unusual circumstances.

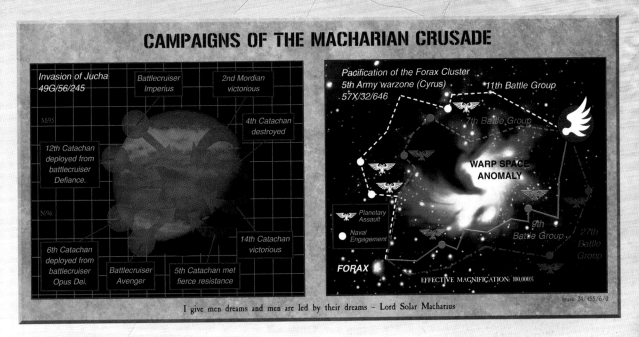

Invasion of Jucha 49G/56/245 · Battlecruiser Imperius · 2nd Mordian victorious · M-95 · 4th Catachan destroyed · 12th Catachan deployed from battlecruiser Defiance. · N-96 · 6th Catachan deployed from battlecruiser Opus Dei. · Battlecruiser Avenger · 5th Catachan met fierce resistance · 14th Catachan victorious

Pacification of the Forax Cluster 5th Army warzone (Cyrus) 57X/32/646 · 11th Battle Group · 7th Battle Group · WARP SPACE ANOMALY · Planetary Assault · Naval Engagement · 9th Battle Group · 27th Battle Group · FORAX · EFFECTIVE MAGNIFICATION: 100.000% · bravo 24/455/6/0

I give men dreams and men are led by their dreams – Lord Solar Macharius

The arbiter and monitor of the tithes is the Departmento Munitorum. This is a colossal organisation represented amongst the High Lords of Terra by the Lord Commander Militant of the Imperial Guard, The Chancellor of the Estate Imperium and The Master of the Administratum. The Departmento Munitorum is responsible for all aspects of the Imperial Guard. It deals with providing training, equipment and supplies for the diverse arms of the Guard. It controls their mustering, transportation to and across war zones, medical and technical support, planning and discipline. Its most impressive facilities are on the garrison worlds established throughout the Imperium, but any world with a substantial tithe obligation will have a Departmento Munitorum presence.

The Departmento Munitorum is organised at the sector and subsector level, and each level has enough autonomy to respond to local problems, normally acting to support Imperial commanders who need aid. They are empowered to raise regiments from worlds close to a crisis point in an increasing radius as required by the crisis. The degree of response will escalate to the level of the threat. If an Imperial world is invaded, the immediate defence will be provided by the Imperial commander and his planetary defence forces. If these are inadequate then the sub-sector command of the Departmento Munitorum will deploy its standing Imperial Guard regiments to augment the local forces. If more forces are needed then the sub-sector command will raise additional troops, initially from nearby worlds and then from any worlds in the sub-sector. As the commitment of troops grows, sector command of the Departmento Munitorum will become involved and reinforcements will be drawn from more and more worlds. The effect is that the harder an enemy strikes the Imperium, the greater the response will be. Central control is not required as the system reacts to the threat posed.

Whilst individual regiments will be commanded by their own officers, normally drawn from the nobility of their home world, when dozens of regiments are mustered then a higher level of command is required. This is provided by the general staff of the Departmento Munitorum. This staff is formed from the best of the officers in the tithed regiments, recommended by their previous service or their family connections, and they receive additional training to prepare them for their greater role in commanding armies. At the highest levels, these men will be known as Lord General Militant or Lord Commander Militant. However, there are

many other titles in regular use. This is rarely a problem as such high appointments are singular in nature with only one Lord General active in a sector at any time.

There are very rare circumstances in which a higher level of command is necessary. This may be the case when a major crusade is being organised and resources from multiple sectors are needed. This rank is that of Warmaster. It is not available to the Departmento Munitorum without the express consent of the High Lords of Terra, and such an individual is said to wield authority bestowed by the Emperor of Mankind Himself. A Warmaster has carte blanche to do what must be done. Because of the unrivalled power of the office, there is rarely more than one active Warmaster in the Imperium, and centuries can pass without one being appointed. The fact that the arch-traitor Horus held the title of Warmaster can, depending on the spirit of the times, stigmatise the bearer of the rank. Other titles have therefore been used, the most famous of these being the rank of Lord Solar, most gloriously held by St Macharius in the early years of the 41st millennium. Some regard a Lord Solar as being of higher rank than even a Warmaster, but to all intents and purposes the titles are interchangeable.

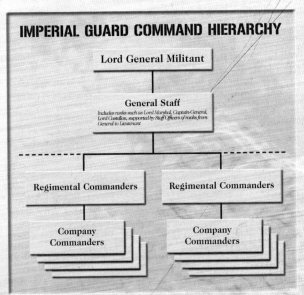

IMPERIAL GUARD COMMAND HIERARCHY

Lord General Militant

General Staff
Includes ranks such as Lord Marshal, Captain-General, Lord Castellan, supported by Staff Officers of ranks from General to Lieutenant.

Regimental Commanders — **Regimental Commanders**

Company Commanders — **Company Commanders**

THE CADIAN 8TH – 'THE LORD CASTELLAN'S OWN'

Shown here are twelve companies (almost 4,000 men) of the 8th Cadian Shock Troop regiment on parade at their Kasr Rorzann castellum. Roughly half of the regiment is present. Of the rest, at least two companies at a time are in hostile environment training on Prosan (the innermost planet of the Cadian system) and two others help to garrison Kasr Sonnen and Kasr Holn (fortress worlds within the Cadian system). In addition, there is always demand for soldiers of the 8th to be indentured to Inquisitors, particularly members of the Cadian Internal Guard, or to assist in training newly-founded regiments.

Each company consists of between two and six platoons of infantry.

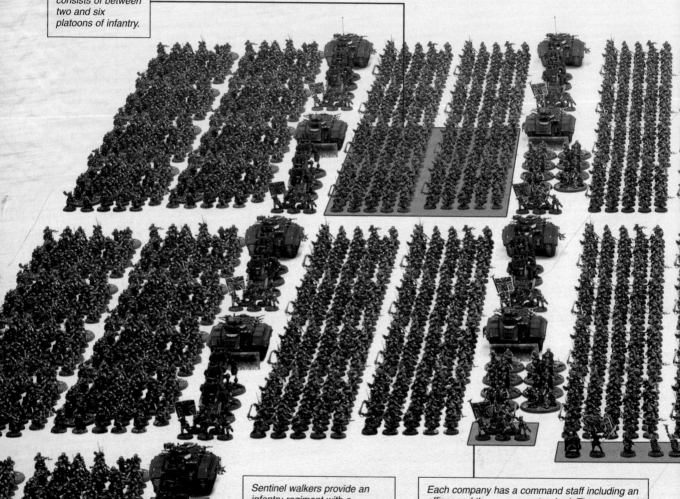

Sentinel walkers provide an infantry regiment with a reconnaissance capability and a degree of fire support.

Each company has a command staff including an officer and the company standard. The command squad may have a number of support squads attached to it.

Sergeant of the 12th company, 1st platoon.

Imperial Guardsman of the 6th company, 3rd platoon.

Cadian Conscript of the 4th company, 2nd platoon.

A platoon of infantry contains a command unit led by a junior officer, normally a Lieutenant. It will then have from two to six squads each consisting of ten Guardsmen.

Each company's command platoon is frequently accompanied by support squads. These are equipped with specialised or heavy weapons, such as missile launchers and mortars. They provide their company with concentrated fire support.

In their teens, Cadians are recruited into Youth Armies which are organised into Whiteshield platoons. These platoons complete their training in proper Shock Troop regiments like the 8th Cadian. As well as learning from the more experienced soldiers, the Whiteshields can prove themselves in the crucible of battle, thus earning the respect and acceptance of the regiment.

An infantry regiment is often supplied with a number of Chimera transports. They allow a commander the option of mounting a number of squads to provide Armoured Fist units for greater tactical flexibility. In addition, they are used to transport command squads which can make good use of the long-range vox casters they carry. Some regiments are entirely mounted in Chimeras but this is relatively rare.

Lord Castellan Ursarkar E. Creed and his assembled command staff. In addition to other officers of the regiment, there will be a number of Commissars assigned to them by the Departmento Munitorum.

Commissar assigned to the command staff of the 8th Cadian Shock Troop regiment.

Ursarkar E. Creed, commander of the Cadian 8th.

THE BATTLE OF TYROK FIELDS

At the outset of the Despoiler's Thirteenth Black Crusade, treachery struck at the heart of the Imperium's defence. As the defenders of the Cadian Gate mustered, the Volscani Cataphracts revealed their true allegiance – to Chaos.

The traitors slaughtered hundreds of loyal Guardsmen before any response could be

coordinated. The intent of the Volscani's treason was revealed as they swarmed aboard the Leviathan command vehicle of the Governor Primus of Cadia. The commander-in-chief of the defenders of the Cadian Gate, present upon the Tyrok Fields to receive the salute of his massed armies, was killed in the brutal attack.

At the darkest moment, the Lord Castellan of Cadia, Ursarkar Creed, took control of the situation. Rallying the glorious 8th, the regiment with which he had made his name, Creed organised the bloodied defenders and ordered the advance upon the traitors.

Accompanied by his trusty retainer, Jarran Kell, bearing the regimental standard of the

Cadian 8th, Creed led the charge into the ranks of the traitorous Volscani. Accompanying the Lord Castellan was the 7th Regiment, whose banner was carried forward by no fewer than twelve separate troopers over the course of the charge, each taking up the standard as its previous bearer fell. The regiment's annals tell that not once was the scarred symbol of the regiment's honour allowed to touch the ground.

Above the battleground strode the mighty Titans of the Legio Ignatum, whose weapons disabled the void shields of the Volscani's Leviathans, enabling Creed's charge to crash home into the ranks of the enemy.

Through Creed's actions, what might have been a grievous defeat for the Imperium, and a nefarious victory for the hordes of Chaos, was turned into a defining moment

for the defenders of Cadia. Though betrayed in the heart of their homelands, the defenders had won the first battle of the Thirteenth Black Crusade. They had no knowledge of what terrible battles were to come, but were certain that the Lord Castellan Ursarkar Creed would be leading them from the fore, at the heart of the fight for the very future of Cadia and of the entire Imperium.

ARMS AND EQUIPMENT OF THE CADIAN 8TH

At the entrance to the Eye of Terror stands the fortress world of Cadia. It stares into the very gates of hell and the courage of its soldiery has repeatedly saved the Imperium from the rampages and depredations of the Legions of Chaos. The soldiers of Cadia form the Shock Troop regiments, famed throughout the Imperium for their skill and discipline. Amongst these most illustrious of regiments the Cadian 8th stands at the fore. Its low designation indicates that it was first founded thousands of years ago and has been re-founded many times since to ensure that its glorious heritage never dies.

Regimental banner of the Cadian 8th Regiment. Imperial Guard Infantry Regiments have two types of standards, regimental and company. Regimental standards are sacred objects, blessed in the greatest cathedral on the Regiments' home world and presented to the regiment on their founding parade. Every great victory of the previous foundings is listed on the banner and predictably its loss is a grave dishonour. Company banners are more mundane, serving to indicate the presence of the company commander and remind the troops of their duty.

The Macharian Cross shown here is much prized by rising officers as it is issued in recognition of intelligent application of the tenets of the Tactica Imperialis. Courage alone will not win this medal and the bearer of one is likely to be recruited into the general staff during future campaigns or crusades when his talents can be developed.

The medal shown is an example of a broad class of gallantry medals referred to as Honorifica Imperialis. These are bestowed within each segmentum so this example would be more properly called the Obscuras Honorifica. The bearer of a Honorifica is a genuine hero of the Imperium and will enjoy the highest regard of his comrades and superiors.

Less prestigious than a Honorifica but more common amongst veterans of the Guard is the Medallion Crimson. This is issued to soldiers who have continued to do their duty despite the most terrible injuries. Often the bearers will also have bionic replacements to show for their courage as well as the Medallion. Most, however, are awarded posthumously.

Shown above are a Cadian Shock Trooper and Kasrkin Grenadier Sergeant from the Cadian 8th Regiment following the Battle of Kasr Tyrok. He carries a Kantrael Amp7 hellpistol. He also carries a sabre of a type normally reserved for officers of armoured regiments. This is probably a trophy taken from the field of battle. The Shock Trooper carries a standard short-pattern lasgun manufactured throughout the Imperium. He has also secured an autopistol as well as affecting a non-standard boot scabbard for his combat knife. This type of unofficial equipment is a more common sight among members of combat engineer special weapons squads.

Standard short pattern lasgun. This weapon was manufactured on Kantrael and, like all similar variants, operates in the nineteen megathule range and can therefore utilise any Departmento Munitorum sanctioned power packs.

Laser technology is reliable and easy to replicate, and although the weapons are not the most powerful they are certainly the most trustworthy. A laser power pack will last for many shots and can be recharged from a standard power source or by exposing its thermal cells to heat or light. In an emergency a pack can be recharged by placing it in a fire, although such treatment tends to shorten the life of the pack and increase the probability of it failing. Many experienced fighters prefer the lasgun over more powerful weapons for these very reasons.

The peaked cap is an option for ranks above sergeant but is generally replaced with a helmet when facing opponents known to utilise snipers. Other ranks in veteran regiments sometimes affect caps instead of helmets but this is frowned on by both Officers and Commissars. The illustration is clearly an officer as he is wearing the distinctive gorget used by Cadian regiments to protect refractor field circuitry.

The standard Cadian tri-dome helmet and mark XI re-breather are fully compatible and provide an excellent defence against most commonly-encountered gasses and pollutants as well as allowing the soldier to operate in airless environments for limited periods. It has also proven useful against plague weapons.

The main types of Cadian shoulder-guard design are shown here. Upon enlistment, squads are issued a unique three-digit squad number. Command squads are issued a two digit number with a central skull motif. Numbers beginning with one or two zeroes are normally reserved for Kasrkin squads or special veteran squads formed from survivors of other squads.

COLLECTING AN IMPERIAL GUARD ARMY

As with any army, the best way to start collecting Imperial Guard is to establish a basic playable force. The force organisation chart shows the minimum selection of units needed to get started. For standard missions, you will need one HQ choice to lead your force and at least two Troops units. While for most armies each slot on the chart represents a single unit, this is not the case with the Imperial Guard. For them, each slot is taken up by a formation which can consist of several units and vehicles.

The photographs below show the core of two Imperial Guard forces, both with the same structure of one HQ choice and two Troops, but using the options within those slots to create distinctive forces. The Cadian army is led by a Command Platoon consisting of a Senior Officer and his Command squad. The basic Troops choices for the army are made up of a standard Infantry Platoon (a Lieutenant and his Command squad accompanied by two Infantry squads) and an Armoured Fist squad with their Chimera APC. In the Catachan army, the Command Platoon has been extended to include a squadron of Sentinels, while this time, both of the basic Troops choices are standard Infantry Platoons.

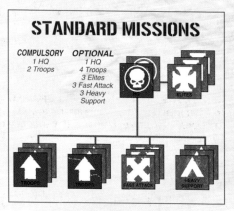

STANDARD MISSIONS

COMPULSORY	OPTIONAL
1 HQ	1 HQ
2 Troops	4 Troops
	3 Elites
	3 Fast Attack
	3 Heavy
	Support

COMMAND PLATOONS

The armies of the Imperial Guard are led by a Senior Officer, supported by his Command Platoon. Normally consisting of the officer himself and his Command squad, he can extend his platoon to include additional support units and advisors if the situation should demand it.

Colonel Renik surveys the advance of his forces from his Command post.

The Command squad is at the heart of an Imperial Guard army. From here the discipline of the army can be held together and the actions of specific units directed through the army vox-casting system.

Under fire from the enemy, Lieutenant Sark issues the order to advance.

The commander of an Imperial Guard army can call upon a variety of specialist advisors. Commissars enhance the discipline of officers and troops alike, while Sanctioned Psykers make use of their power to defend the army from the psychic assaults of the enemy. The Priests of the Ecclesiarchy may also be called upon to inspire the men to acts of bravery.

SUPPORT SQUADS

In the ruins at the edge of a forest, a sniper trains his sights on a Tau Devilfish commander.

With its Heavy and Special Weapons teams, the Command Platoon contains some of the most powerful weapons in an Imperial Guard army, all under the direct control of the commanding officer.

Heavy and Special Weapons squads hold the line as the Sentinels surge forward.

Alongside these squads, the army commander can rely on a small squadron of Sentinels to provide fast moving firepower and reconnaissance.

While the majority of an Imperial Guard army is made up of standard Infantry squads, there are a number of highly trained, specialist units and abhuman auxiliaries at the Senior Officer's disposal.

Storm Troopers pour from their Chimera tank to confront the forces of Abaddon's Black Legion.

Better trained, armed and armoured than regular Guardsmen, Storm Troopers can infiltrate ahead of the rest of the army, or be dropped into the midst of the enemy's lines during the battle.

The brutal Ogryns charge out to meet the mutated hordes of Chaos, while the elite of the Imperial Guard hold the line.

Ratling Snipers infiltrate themselves into effective sniping positions before battle commences, whilst Ogryns are commonly

Enginseer Gant inspects his charges before the Battle for Hive Infernus.

Tech-Priest Enginseers in battle use the arcane lore of technology to repair the fighting machines of the Imperial Guard.

deployed in the front lines where their great strength and savagery in assaults could win the day.

TROOPS

The core of an Imperial Guard army consists of a number of different infantry formations. The most common of these is the standard Infantry Platoon, made up of a number of separate Infantry units united by a single Command squad. These can be supported by less flexible platoons of Conscripts and the mechanised Armoured Fist squads.

Lieutenant Harker leads his platoon through the dense jungles of Piscina V.

The basic Infantry Platoons of the Imperial Guard offer both strength in numbers and a wide range of weapons options.

A squad of the Cadian 8th prepare for the defence of Kasr Tyrok.

Deep in the desert, a unit of the 12th Tallarns wait in ambush.

A platoon of Conscripts charge out into no man's land from the safety of their trenches.

A Chimera APC provides cover for an Armoured Fist unit as they cautiously advance through a ruined building.

Conscript Platoons can be used where superior numbers are more important than training.

Armoured Fist units lend speed and tactical flexibility to the often slow and rigid infantry formations of the Imperial Guard.

Elements of the 21st Mordian Iron Guard fight for the city of Vanandra.

Warriors of 93rd Valhallan regiment brave the frozen tundra of their homeworld.

HEAVY SUPPORT

An infantry charge would be a costly affair without the firepower of whole platoons of heavy weapons and large numbers of Leman Russ and Basilisk tanks providing support.

Variants of the Leman Russ battle tank offer a combination of heavy armour and ordnance, while the Basilisk tank provides long-range artillery, capable of firing into enemy positions over intervening terrain.

Ork Tankbustas launch a suicidal attack on an approaching wave of Imperial tanks.

Mortar team

Autocannon team

Heavy bolter team

Lascannon team

In Infantry Platoons, Heavy Weapons teams boost the firepower of the Infantry squads. Organising these teams into dedicated Heavy Weapons Platoons allows that concentrated firepower to be more easily directed.

FAST ATTACK

Elements of Imperial Guard forces move ahead of the bulk of the army to launch flank attacks or scout out enemy positions.

Sentinels mainly function as scouts, moving ahead of the lumbering tank and infantry formations. The range of different weapon fits available for the Sentinel allow it to operate in a number of additional roles.

Cadian pattern – The Cadian pattern Sentinel is armed with an autocannon, making it effective against light-to-medium armoured vehicles and armoured infantry. The Sentinel shown here has also been upgraded with extra armour.

Catachan pattern – The heavy flamer on a Catachan pattern Sentinel is most useful against tightly packed infantry, whether on open ground or in cover.

Mars pattern – The Mars pattern Sentinel carries a multi-laser, making it effective against lightly armoured vehicles and infantry.

Armageddon pattern – The Armageddon pattern Sentinel comes with a lascannon, making it ideally suited to the role of tank-hunter. This Sentinel has also been given an armoured crew compartment.

An Imperial advance force moves rapidly through the ruins of a hive city, guided by a squadron of Sentinel Scouts.

The Hellhound tank is fitted with an Inferno cannon, making it effective against enemy infantry and light vehicles in entrenched positions, while Rough Rider units make ideal fast flanking units.

PAINTING TANKS

The camouflage patterns on the tanks of the Imperial Guard reflect the terrain in which they will be deployed. This is a guide to painting the tanks of the Cadian 121st in their Cadian temperate zone pattern.

ARMY BADGE

We used a transfer to apply the army badge of the Cadian army to the right face of the turret.

LIGHT CAMO

- We began with a basecoat of Kommando Khaki, followed by a highlight of Kommando Khaki mixed with Skull White.

TANK NUMBER

The tank number that we added to both sides of the tank was also a transfer.

DARK CAMO

- We started with a basecoat of Dark Angels Green, then drybrushed Catachan Green and Camo Green as highlights.

GLASS

- The glass section was painted with a basecoat of Regal Blue.

- A highlight of Enchanted Blue was applied.

- Fortress Grey was then added to the Enchanted Blue for a final highlight.

- A small dot of Skull White in the corner helped to create the impression of a reflection on the glass.

CHIPPED ARMOUR

- The area of the chipping was painted with Tin Bitz, followed by a layer of Chainmail.

TANK TRACKS

- The tracks were undercoated with Tin Bitz, then we drybrushed the tracks with Boltgun Metal.

The defenders of Command Bunker 135 advance to meet the charge of the Black Legion.

REGIMENTS OF THE IMPERIAL GUARD

There are millions of Imperial Guard regiments, all with their own distinctive uniforms. Many of these regiments employ different camouflage schemes depending on the nature of the terrain in which they will be fighting.

OFFICERS

Among the millions of officers that lead the forces of the Imperial Guard across the galaxy, there are some whose deeds set them apart from their peers.

Ursarkar E. Creed and Jarran Kell

Commissar Yarrick

Captain Chenkov

Captain Al'rahem

93rd Valhallan
Soldane Campaign, M38

- ● Bubonic Brown
- ● Chaos Black

211th Mordian
Capital Garrison, M38

- ● Enchanted Blue
- ● Blazing Orange

17th Catachan
'Screaming Devils'

- ○ Rotting Flesh
- ● Dark Angels Green

12th Tallarn
Cursus War, M40

- ● Bestial Brown
- ● Bronzed Flesh

23rd Valhallan
Steppe Fatigues

- ● Dark Angels Green
- ● Desert Yellow

56th Mordian
Mechanised Infantry Uniform

- ● Codex Grey
- ● Chaos Black

391st Catachan
'Coiling Cobras'

- ● Bubonic Brown
- ● Bestial Brown

89th Tallarn
Annukani Campaign, M39

- ● Codex Grey
- ● Chaos Black

11th Kado
Ash Waste Camouflage

- ● Shadow Grey
- ● Codex Grey

2nd Desedniain
Dress Uniform, M41

- ● Blood Red
- ○ Skull White

898th Cromaryn
Vanryan's World Cleansing

- ● Codex Grey
- ● Chaos Black

35th Orcallian
Salt Desert Campaign, M40

- ○ Bleached Bone
- ● Space Wolves Grey

Even though the forces of a single world maintain the same basic uniform, there is a still a great diversity in camouflage schemes between different regiments and theatres of war. In the wider Imperium, a successful uniform design may also be found amongst the forces of other worlds.

8th Cadian
Standard Fatigues pre-M38
- Catachan Green
- Desert Yellow

8th Cadian
Winter Fatigues, M41
- Skull White
- Shadow Grey

8th Cadian
Jungle Fatigues post-M39
- Bestial Brown
- Catachan Green

8th Cadian
Vrakesworld Campaign, M38
- Scorched Brown
- Bleached Bone

8th Cadian
Gerreck Heresy, M40
- Bubonic Brown
- Bestial Brown

122nd Cadian
Winter Campaign on
Vintock III, M40
- Fortress Grey
- Space Wolves Grey

110th Cadian 'Shadow Corps'
Purging of Shaboloth
Night World, M41
- Chaos Black
- Catachan Green

512th Cadian
Cadian Orbital Defence
Detail, M41
- Codex Grey
- Chaos Black

39th Cadian 'Xenobane'
Chincare Hrud
Infestation, M41
- Catachan Green
- Dark Angels Green

450th Cadian
Klestry Forest War, M40
- Catachan Green
- Goblin Green

39th Cadian
Veldt Fatigues, M41
- Terracotta
- Graveyard Earth

122nd Cadian
Battle for Vogen, M41
- Shadow Grey
- Chaos Black

**180th Cadian
'Stalking Tigers'**
Standard Fatigues (adopted M40)
- Dark Angels Green
- Graveyard Earth

180th Cadian 'Stalking Tigers'
Rassagar III Campaign, M41
(Defeat of Waaagh! Craslash)
- Camo Green
- Tanned Flesh

85th Cadian 'Firedrakes'
Gorsinian Lava Desert
Campaign, M39
- Terracotta
- Red Gore

101st Vendoland
Spring Offensive, M41
(Third War for Gassharma)
- Catachan Green
- Camo Green

**31st Harakoni
Warhawks 'Helldivers'**
Dress Fatigues, M41
- Kommando Khaki
- Chaos Black

182nd Moloch Rifles
Maugral Prime Campaign
- Scorched Brown
- Kommando Khaki

4th Brimlock Dragoons
Operation Hydra
Damocles Gulf Crusade
- Bestial Brown
- Kommando Khaki

51st Coronan Grenadiers
Polar Fatigues, M41
- Bleached Bone
- Graveyard Earth

PAINTING THE CADIA 8TH

There is a huge variety of regimental colours amongst the armies of the Imperial Guard. This is a guide to painting Imperial Guard in the home garrison uniform of the Cadian 8th Regiment.

SKIN

- We started with a basecoat of Dwarf Flesh then added
- a layer of Elf Flesh.

FATIGUES

- Begin with a basecoat of Desert Yellow then add a
- highlight layer to the cloth of an equal parts mix of Desert Yellow and Bleached Bone.

BODY ARMOUR

- We began by applying a basecoat of Catachan Green, followed by an
- extreme highlight of Camo Green.

LEATHER

- A basecoat of Chaos Black was applied,
- followed by a highlight of Codex Grey.

UNIT NUMBER

The unit number on the uniform of the Cadian 8th is a three-digit number. We used a transfer, applied to the left shoulder pad.

GUN METAL

- Boltgun Metal was used as a basecoat, then the
- metal was drybrushed with Chainmail.

ARMY BADGE

The army badge on the right shoulder of the uniform of our Cadian 8th is a transfer of a graphic representing the Cadian Gate.

DETAILS

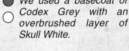

- We used a basecoat of Codex Grey with an
- overbrushed layer of Skull White.

APPLYING TRANSFERS

0.30

The officer shares the same uniform colours as the regular infantry, but with added gold details.

Begin with a basecoat of Tin Bitz, then add a highlight of Shining Gold.

The Conscripts are distinguished by a stripe running from the front to the back of their helmets.

Carefully paint the stripe using Skull White onto the finished helmet.

The camouflage pattern of the Kasrkin has extra patches of colour added.

Add a jagged shape with Bleached Bone then fill the shape in with Vermin Brown leaving a Bleached Bone border.

For a wealth of useful techniques and ideas about painting your models, read How to Paint Citadel Miniatures.

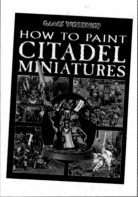

Lord Martial Graf Harazahn dictates the battle orders at the Gates of Balcarhsa

IMPERIAL GUARD ARMOURY

Imperial Guard characters may have two weapons, of which only one may be two-handed. In addition, each Senior Officer may have up to 100 points of items from the Wargear section of the Armoury; other models allowed to choose equipment from the Armoury may purchase up to 50 points of wargear. You may not take duplicate items for the same model but may have more than one master-crafted weapon. All weapons and wargear must be represented on the model.

SINGLE-HANDED WEAPONS

Bolt pistol . . . . .1 point

Plasma pistol . . . . .10 points

Power fist . . . . .20 points
Officers only

Power weapon . . . . .5 points
Officers, Priests, Rough Rider Sgts & Storm Trooper Sgts only

Force weapon . . . . .25 points
Sanctioned Psyker only

Close combat weapon . . . . . . .1 point

TWO-HANDED WEAPONS

Bolter . . . . .1 point

Eviscerator . . . . .25 points
Priests only

Shotgun . . . . .1 point

Storm bolter . . . . .5 points

WARGEAR

Bionics . . . . .5 points

Carapace armour . . . . .5 points

Frag grenades . . . . .1 point

Holy relic . . . . .30 points
Priests only, no more than one per army

Honorifica Imperialis . . . . . . .25 points
No more than one per army

Krak grenades . . . . .2 points

Macharian cross . . . . .20 points
Officers only

Master-crafted weapon . . . . . .15 points

Medallion Crimson . . . . .15 points

Melta bombs . . . . .5 points

Purity seals . . . . .5 points
Priests only

Refractor field . . . . .15 points
Officers, Enginseers only

Regimental standard . . . . . . .20 points
Standard Bearer only

Rosarius . . . . .25 points
Priests only

Servitor . . . . .varies
Enginseer only

Signum . . . . .15 points
Enginseer Only

Surveyor . . . . .2 points

Trademark item . . . . .10 points
Officers only

Bionics

These allow an Imperial Guard character who has suffered a crippling injury to return to service but they do not improve his abilities in any way.

However, there is a chance that an attack will damage a bionic part rather than doing any real harm. To represent this, if a model with bionics is killed, instead of removing it place it on its side. Roll a D6 at the start of the next turn: on a roll of 6 the model is stood back up with 1 wound but on any other roll it is removed as a casualty.

Carapace Armour

Carapace armour is made up of large rigid plates of armaplas or ceramite moulded to fit parts of the body. This provides better protection than the flak armour which is normally worn by the Imperial Guard. A model that has carapace armour receives a 4+ Armour save.

Company Standard

Units of Imperial Guard infantry (not including Conscripts, Enginseers, Ogryns, Ratlings or Storm Troopers) with a model within 12" of the standard can re-roll failed Morale tests.

Eviscerator

The Eviscerator is a two-handed chainsword capable of inflicting horrific injuries on living creatures, slicing through walls and even damaging vehicles. It counts as a power fist in all respects except that, because it is a two-handed weapon, the wielder cannot use it in combination with another close combat weapon and rolls 2D6 + Strength when penetrating armour.

Demolition charge

A model armed with a demolition charge may use it in the Shooting phase instead of making its normal shooting attack.

Demolition charges have a range of 6". The attack is treated the same way as for an ordnance attack, except that the model throwing the charge can move on the turn that it throws. Place the large Ordnance Blast marker as you would normally and then roll to see if the charge scatters (due to its extremely short range a demolition charge is almost as dangerous for the user as it is for the target!).

Demolition charges are one-shot weapons. If a model uses his demolition charge, replace him with a model armed with the basic weapon for the squad. If one is unavailable, the model is removed instead.

	Range	Str	AP	Notes
Demolition Charge	6"	8	2	Ordnance blast

May move and fire, one shot only, uses large Ordnance template.

Holy Relic

A model bearing a holy relic may reveal it once per battle. This may be done at any time, as long as the model with the relic does not move on the turn it is shown.

On the turn the relic is revealed, all friendly models that are within 2D6" get a +1 Attack bonus for the rest of that turn. The relic may be revealed in an opposing player's turn if you wish.

Honorifica Imperialis

This award is one of the highest honours that can be won by all ranks in the Imperial Guard. Whatever the original status of the bearer he will use the same profile as a Heroic Senior Officer. He will not become an independent character or an Officer as a result but will continue in his original role, albeit with better characteristics. The Honorifica Imperialis can be bestowed on Techpriest Enginseers, Priests and other characters in the list that are not Guardsmen per se, in which case it is termed the Honorifica Imperialis Mundanus.

Macharian Cross

The Cross is awarded only to Imperial Guard Officers in recognition of innovative and successful tactical thinking. The bearer can be expected to use his initiative in battle. After deployment is complete (including deploying infiltrators and moving scouts) but before determining who has the first turn, any single Infantry squad (including Hardened Veterans, Storm Troopers, Ogryns, Ratlings, Infantry Platoon squads and Armoured Fist squads, but not any vehicles) within 6" of the Officer may be redeployed up to 12", but must abide by all the mission's deployment zones and rules.

Master-crafted Weapons

A master-crafted weapon follows the normal rules for the converted weapon except that it allows one failed to hit roll per turn to be re-rolled. Such a modified weapon is taken as an upgrade for a weapon already carried by a model and must be represented by a suitably ornate weapon on the model itself. A grenade cannot be master-crafted.

The upgrade cost of 15 points is added to the normal cost of the weapon but only the upgrade cost is taken against the points limit on wargear taken by a model (so a master-crafted power weapon costs 20 points but counts as only 15 points against a character's Wargear limit).

Master-Vox

The vox-caster attached to the army's Command HQ is the hub of all communications into, through and out of the Company. It can be upgraded to a master-vox, a far more sophisticated version capable of maintaining several channels simultaneously. Any number of squads may use the Leadership of the HQ's Officer for a single Morale or Leadership test per turn rather than the usual limit of one allowed with a Vox-caster.

Medallion Crimson

This medal is awarded to men who have suffered the most horrific injuries and have not lost their faith in the Emperor or their will to fight on. It takes a lot to stop a man who has earned this decoration. The first time the bearer is wounded by an attack that causes instant death he takes a single wound instead.

Medi-pack

Medi-packs (also referred to as Narthecium) allow a unit with a medic to ignore the first failed saving throw it rolls in every turn. The medi-pack may not be used on any model which suffers instant death (see the Warhammer 40,000 rulebook) or that has been hit by a close combat weapon that allows no Armour save. The medi-pack may not be used if the medic is in base contact with an enemy model.

Purity Seals

If a model wearing purity seals falls back, roll one extra D6 for Fall Back distance (usually 3D6 instead of 2D6), and then discard the dice of your choice before seeing how far they fall back. If a model with purity seals is part of a unit then this ability applies to the whole unit, not just the model with the purity seals.

Refractor Field

This piece of equipment produces an energy field that gives the model a 5+ Invulnerable save. This may be used instead of the model's normal Armour save.

Regimental Standard

Units of Imperial Guard (not including Conscripts, Enginseers, Ogryns, Ratlings or Storm Troopers) near the regimental standard fight with greater fervour. Add +1 to combat resolution of any assault that takes place at least partly within 6" of the regimental standard (ie, treat the Imperial Guard side as having scored one more wound). A Regimental Standard also counts as a Company Standard (see Company Standard entry for further details).

Rosarius

A rosarius is a badge of faith incorporating a powerful conversion field that protects its wearer. A model with a rosarius gets a 4+ Invulnerable save that may be taken instead of the model's normal Armour save.

Servitor

A Techpriest Enginseer may be accompanied by up to four Servitors. Together they will form a unit. The Servitors may be the same or different types as desired. The types are as follows:

- Technical Servitors are a common sight in the Imperium. They are not really intended for combat, but are very useful in repairing battlefield equipment, as explained in the Techpriest Enginseer army list entry. Other Servitor types may not help repair battlefield equipment.

- Combat Servitors are intended to fight in close combat so are equipped with a power fist and a close combat weapon.

- Gun Servitors are intended to provide fire support for the Techpriest Enginseer while he works. They are armed with one of the following weapons at the cost indicated: multi-melta at +25 pts; heavy bolter at +15 pts; plasma cannon at +35 pts. Only one plasma cannon-armed Gun-servitor can accompany each Techpriest Enginseer.

	Pts/model	WS	BS	S	T	W	I	A	Ld	Sv
Gun Servitor	10+gun	3	4	3	3	1	3	1	8	4+
Combat Servitor	25	4	3	3	3	1	3	1	8	4+
Technical Servitor	10	3	3	3	3	1	3	1	8	5+

Servo-arm

Many Techpriest Enginseers are equipped with a powerful servo-arm, primarily to make battlefield repairs. The servo-arm makes a single power fist attack in close combat, hitting on a 4+, independently of the Techpriest Enginseer's attacks.

Signum

This is a special form of communication device that allows the Techpriest Enginseer to access a myriad of useful battlefield targeting information, and then pass it on to his companions. In game terms it allows you, each turn, to re-roll one missed to hit shooting roll for the Techpriest Enginseer or his attendant Servitors.

Surveyor

A surveyor is used to detect hidden enemy troops. If enemy infiltrators set up within 4D6" of a model with a surveyor then the model is allowed to take a 'free' shot at them (or sound the alarm in a Raid scenario). If the model is part of a unit, the whole unit may shoot. These shots are taken before the battle begins and may cause the infiltrators to fall back.

Targeter

Models equipped with a targeter are allowed to pre-measure the range to a target before they decide who to shoot at in the Shooting phase. After you have used a targeter then any 'Guess' range weapons may not be fired that turn (this rule is included to avoid players using their targeters to gain advantages for other units that don't have them).

Trademark Item

This is something the character carries into battle to show his disregard for the enemy. It could be a swagger stick or a nonchalantly smoked cigar, or something more grandiose like a billowing, scarlet cape or a loyal pet.

A unit led in person by a character who carries a trademark item will be reassured by his presence and may re-roll any failed Morale or Pinning checks that it suffers. However, if the character is slain, the unit must pass a Morale test to avoid falling back.

Vox-caster

Communications between Imperial Guard units on the battlefield are dealt with by troopers trained to use special comm-links. The size and appearance of a vox-caster depends on its place of origin but in game terms they all have the same effects.

If a Command HQ or Command Section has a vox-caster, then one squad per turn that also has a vox-caster may use the Leadership value of the Officer, no matter where they are located on the battlefield (ie, they don't have to be within 12" of the Officer as would normally be the case). You may choose to use the vox-caster at any time (eg, when an eligible squad is about to take a Leadership test, even if the Command unit is in reserve). The benefits of standards and trademark items are not conveyed through the vox-caster!

VEHICLE UPGRADES

Imperial Guard vehicles may be fitted with the following equipment. Upgrades marked with * cannot be used by Sentinels, otherwise all upgrades can be used by all vehicles in the army list. Any upgrades taken must be shown on the model. No upgrade can be used more than once on a single vehicle and no vehicle can include more than one pintle-mounted weapon.

Armoured crew compartment . . . . 15 points for Sentinel
20 points otherwise

Camo netting . . . . .1 point

Extra armour . . . . .5 points

Hunter-killer missile .10 points

Improved comms . . . . .20 points

Mine sweeper* . . . . .5 points

Pintle storm bolter* .10 points

Pintle heavy stubber* . . . . .12 points

Rough terrain modification . . . . .5 points

Searchlight . . . . .1 point

Smoke launchers . . . . .3 points

Track guards* . . . . .10 points

NOTES

Pintle heavy stubber profile is range 36", Strength 4, AP6, Heavy 3. It may be fired in the same way as a pintle storm bolter.

Armoured Crew Compartment

These may only be added to open-topped vehicles. The vehicle no longer counts as being open-topped.

Camo Netting

Vehicles often carry rolls of camouflage netting that can be unrolled to help hide the vehicle. In scenarios using the Hidden Set-up rules, vehicles carrying camo netting can be set up hidden anywhere in their deployment zone, not just in or behind appropriate terrain features.

Extra Armour

Vehicles equipped with extra armour count 'Crew Stunned' results on the Damage tables as 'Crew Shaken' results instead.

Hunter-killer Missile

These missiles are treated as krak missiles with an unlimited range but may be used only once per battle. Roll to hit and wound or to penetrate armour as normal.

Mine Sweeper

The vehicle is fitted with a heavy dozer blade or some other device designed to clear minefields (see the Warhammer 40,000 rulebook). It can enter a minefield without being attacked. Any minefield that the vehicle moves across is cleared and removed from play.

Improved Comms

These upgrades take the form of long 'whip' aerials or other large aerial set-ups. A vehicle with improved comms can communicate with other Imperial Guard formations, such as nearby reserves or artillery support. To represent this, the improved comms allow the Imperial Guard player to re-roll one Reserves roll per turn, and to re-roll the dice when checking to see if an enemy unit or obstacle is hit by a preliminary bombardment.

Pintle Storm Bolter/Heavy Stubber

Pintle-mounted weapons are located on the outside of a vehicle and can be used by a crewman from an open hatch or by remote control from inside. A pintle weapon can be fired when the vehicle is eligible to fire another non-ordnance weapon.

Rough Terrain Modification

This is a catch-all category for the many upgrades that help vehicles move through difficult terrain, such as dozer blades. They allow a vehicle moving no further than 6" that turn to re-roll a failed Difficult Terrain test.

Searchlight

Searchlights can be used in missions where the rules for night fighting are used (see page 134 of the Warhammer 40,000 rules). They allow one enemy unit spotted by the vehicle to be fired at by any other Imperial Guard units in range that have a line of fire. However, a vehicle that uses a searchlight can be fired at by any enemy units in their next turn; they can see the light shining in the dark.

Smoke Launchers

These carry charges that can be fired to hide the vehicle behind a cloud of smoke. Once per game, after completing movement (no matter how far), a vehicle with smoke launchers can trigger them. Place cotton wool around the vehicle to show it is concealed by smoke. The vehicle cannot fire and use its smoke launchers in the same turn. Any penetrating hits scored by the enemy in their next Shooting phase count as glancing hits. After the enemy's turn, the smoke disperses with no further effect. Note that a vehicle may still use smoke launchers even if its crew are stunned or shaken.

Track Guards

Track guards protect the vulnerable track mechanism of an armoured vehicle. The vehicle treats 'Immobilised' results as 'Crew Stunned' instead, on a D6 roll of 4+. This result applies even if the vehicle has extra armour.

IMPERIAL GUARD ARMY LIST

This section of the book is given over to the Imperial Guard army list, a listing of the different troops and vehicles an Imperial Guard Commander can use in battle, or in your case, games of Warhammer 40,000. The army list allows you to fight battles using the scenarios included in the Warhammer 40,000 rulebook, but it also provides you with the basic information you'll require to field an Imperial Guard army in scenarios you've devised yourself, or as part of a campaign series of games, or whatever else may take your fancy.

The army list is split into five sections. All of the squads, vehicles and characters in an army list are placed in one of the five sections depending upon their role on the battlefield. In addition every model included in the army list is given a points value, which varies depending upon how effective that model is on the battlefield.

Before you can choose an army for a game you will need to agree with your opponent upon a scenario and upon the total number of points each of you will spend on your army. Having done this you can proceed to pick an army as described below.

Using A Force Organisation Chart

The army lists are used in conjunction with the Force Organisation chart from a scenario. Each Force Organisation chart is split into five categories that correspond to the sections in the army list, and each category has one or more boxes. Each box indicates that you may make one choice from that section of the army list, while a dark toned box means that you <u>must</u> make a choice from that section.

Using The Army Lists

To make a choice, look in the relevant section in the army list and decide what unit you wish to have in your army, how many models there will be in the unit, and which upgrades you want (if any). Remember that you cannot field models that are equipped with weapons and wargear that are not shown on the model.

Once this is done subtract the points value of the unit from your total points, and then go back and make another choice. Continue doing this until you have spent all your points. Now you are ready to do battle!

Army List Entries

Each army list entry consists of the following:

Unit Name: The type of unit, which may also show a limitation on the minimum or maximum number of choices you can make of that unit type (0-1, for example).

Profile: These are the characteristics of that unit type, including its points cost. Where the unit has different warriors, there may be more than one profile.

Number/Squad: This shows the number of models in the unit, or the number of models you may take for one choice from the Force Organisation chart. Often this is a variable amount, in which case it shows the minimum and maximum unit size.

Weapons: These are the unit's standard weapons.

Options: This lists the different weapon and equipment options for the unit and any additional points cost for taking these options. If a squad is allowed to have models with upgrades, then these must be given to ordinary team members, not the character.

Special Rules: This is where you'll find any special rules that apply to the unit.

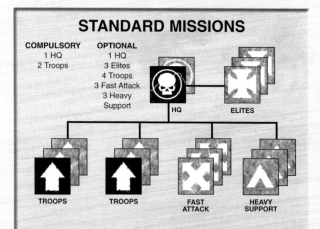

STANDARD MISSIONS

COMPULSORY	OPTIONAL
1 HQ	1 HQ
2 Troops	3 Elites
	4 Troops
	3 Fast Attack
	3 Heavy Support

HQ ELITES

TROOPS   TROOPS   FAST ATTACK   HEAVY SUPPORT

The Standard Missions Force Organisation chart is a good example of how to choose an army. To begin with you will need at least one HQ unit and two Troops units (dark shaded boxes indicate units that must be taken for the mission). This leaves the following for you to choose from to make up your army's total points value: Up to 1 additional HQ unit, 0-3 additional Elite units, 0-4 additional Troops units, 0-3 additional Fast Attack units, 0-3 additional Heavy Support units.

HQ

The Tactica Imperium normally uses specific titles to refer Officer ranks; Junior Officers are listed as Lieutenants, senior Officers are named as Captains or Colonels. In practice, the Imperial Guard is drawn from so many different worlds, many of which speak varying dialects – or even totally different languages – so that the actual titles applied to officers can vary wildly.

Those soldiers demonstrating an affinity with specialised weaponry are gathered together in squads to provide fire support for the normal Imperial Guard platoons.

Fire Support squads are used to suppress enemy infantry formations and to take out light vehicles such as skimmers and buggies.

Anti-tank squads are equipped with the heaviest man-portable weapons in the regiment and are invaluable in providing defence against enemy armoured vehicles and large alien creatures.

Anti-personnel weapons, mortars are ideal for laying down a hail of suppressive fire that can pin infantry formations in place. They are also able to fire indirectly, lobbing their shells over woods or hills to strike at foes who would otherwise be hidden.

☠ 1 COMMAND PLATOON ☠

A Command Platoon consists of a Command squad and 0-5 Support squads.

Support squads can be Anti-tank squads, Mortar squads, Fire Support squads, Special Weapons squads and Sentinel squadrons, as listed below.

COMMAND SQUAD

	Pts/Model	WS	BS	S	T	W	I	A	Ld	Sv
Heroic Senior Officer	70	4	4	3	3	3	4	3	9	5+
Senior Officer	55	4	4	3	3	2	4	3	8	5+
Junior Officer	40	3	3	3	3	1	3	2	8	5+
Veteran	+6	3	3	3	3	1	3	2	8	5+
Guardsman	–	3	3	3	3	1	3	1	7	5+

Number/squad: A Command squad consists of one Officer, chosen from the list above, and a personal staff of four Guardsmen. The Officer's points cost includes the basic cost of his staff.

Weapons: Officers carry a laspistol and a close combat weapon. Guardsmen are armed with either a lasgun, or a laspistol and a close combat weapon.

Character: The Officer is an independent character. However, he must remain within 2" of his Command squad at all times and may not leave it. If it is wiped out, the Officer reverts to being an independent character.

Options: All Officers have access to the Imperial Guard Armoury.

The Guardsmen can be equipped with frag grenades at +1 pt per model and/or krak grenades at +2 pts per model.

Two Guardsmen may form a single heavy weapon crew. A heavy weapon crew must be armed with one of the weapons from the following list:

• Lascannon at +25 pts; autocannon at +15 pts; missile launcher at +15 pts; mortar at +10 pts; heavy bolter at +10 pts.

0-2 Fire Support Squad ....35 pts + heavy weapons

Number/squad: Six Guardsmen forming three heavy weapon crews. See the Command Squad entry for Guardsman profile.

Weapons: Lasguns. Each heavy weapon crew must be equipped with either a heavy bolter at +15 pts or an autocannon at +20 pts.

0-2 Anti-tank Support Squad ....35 pts + heavy weapons

Number/squad: Six Guardsmen forming three heavy weapon crews. See the Command Squad entry for Guardsman profile.

Weapons: Lasguns. Each heavy weapon crew must be equipped with either a lascannon at +25 pts or a missile launcher at +20 pts.

0-2 Mortar Support Squad ....80 pts

Number/squad: Lasguns. Six Guardsmen forming three heavy weapon crews. See the Command Squad entry for Guardsman profile.

Weapons: Each heavy weapon crew is equipped with a mortar.

No more than two Support squads of each type (or one in the case of Sentinel squadrons) may be used.

A Command Platoon counts as a single unit for army selection, deployment and reserves purposes. However, each sub-unit may deploy or arrive in a different location and act independently.

The most senior officer of an Imperial Guard army leads the men of his company from a command squad. He directs their actions and commands its most powerful weapons. He is in constant communication with his subordinates, coordinating attacks and providing a solid anchor of leadership.

Any Guardsman not acting as heavy weapon crew may be armed with one of the special weapons from the following list:

• meltagun at +10 pts; plasma gun at +10 pts; grenade launcher at +8 pts; flamer at +6 pts.

One Guardsman not acting as heavy weapon crew or using a special weapon may be equipped with a vox-caster at +5 pts. In the the case of the Command Squad of the Command Platoon, the the vox-caster may be upgraded to a master-vox for a further +20 pts.

Character: Any Guardsmen not using special weapons, a vox-caster or forming a heavy weapon crew may be upgraded to be a Veteran at +6 pts, and will have access to the Imperial Guard Armoury.

Up to two Veterans may select one of the following further upgrades:

• Standard Bearer at +5 pts. The Veteran carries the company banner. Only a Command Squad acting as part of the Command Platoon may have a Standard Bearer.

• Medic at +5 pts. The Veteran is equipped with a medi-pack.

Transport: The Command squad and its Officer may be mounted in a Chimera transport vehicle at +70 pts. See the Chimera transport entry on page 45 for more details.

SPECIAL RULE

Leadership: Any Imperial Guard unit within 12" of the Officer may use his Leadership when taking Morale and Leadership tests as long as he isn't in close combat, falling back or pinned.

The regiment's most competent soldiers are formed into a command squad, and these men are often equipped with specialised equipment or given extra training to enable them to function as medics or vox-operators. Often, a soldier who has displayed gallantry above and beyond the call of duty may be permitted to carry the regimental standard.

0-1 Sentinel Support Squadron

One Sentinel squadron may be selected, using the unit size, options and upgrades listed on page 47.

0-2 Special Weapons Support Squad.........35 pts + weapons

Number/squad: Six Guardsmen

Weapons: Lasgun or laspistol and close combat weapon. See the Command Squad entry for Guardsman profile.

Up to 3 Guardsmen can replace their weaponry with a weapon from the following list (however, only one may carry a demolition charge):

• meltagun at +15 pts; flamer at +9 pts; grenade launcher at +12 pts; sniper rifle at +10 pts; demolition charge at +10 pts.

Options: The entire squad can be equipped with frag grenades at +1 pt per model, krak grenades at +2 pts per model, or meltabombs at +5 pts per model.

These sombre and solitary individuals are able to use their psychic powers to advise the senior officers of their regiment. They can augment the officer's ability to command, protect him from psychic attack or, in the direst circumstances, fire bolts of lightning from their hands.

☠ 0-5 SANCTIONED PSYKERS ☠

	Pts/Model	WS	BS	S	T	W	I	A	Ld	Sv
Sanctioned Psyker	12	2	2	3	3	1	3	1	8	5+

Number/squad: You may include up to five Sanctioned Psykers in your army. These do not count as one of your HQ choices and may be taken in addition to your usual allocation of HQ units in a mission. Each Psyker must join a separate unit in the army as described below.

Weapons: Laspistol and close combat weapon.

Options: Sanctioned Psykers have access to the Imperial Guard Armoury.

SPECIAL RULES

Advisors: See the rules in the box to the left.

It's For Your Own Good!: If a Sanctioned Psyker is attached to a unit which contains a Commissar and suffers a Perils of the Warp attack while using a psychic power, the Commissar will immediately execute him to prevent him being possessed. Remove the Psyker model as a casualty. The power he was attempting to use does not work.

Psychic Powers: The Psyker has one Psychic ability, selected at random by rolling a dice and consulting the table below.

SANCTIONED PSYKER POWERS

D6 Power

1 No usable power. The Sanctioned Psyker is disturbed by waking Warp-spawned nightmares and does not dare to use his abilities at this time.

2 Telepathic order. This power allows the Sanctioned Psyker to extend the zone of influence of an Officer he is accompanying. Use at the start of the Imperial Guard turn. If the test is passed, the Leadership radius of any Officer in the same squad as the Sanctioned Psyker who used the power is extended to 18" until the start of the next Imperial Guard turn.

3 Psychic ward. Sanctioned Psykers are particularly useful in countering the heretical abilities of aliens and traitor scum. If a psychic power would normally affect the Sanctioned Psyker or the unit he is accompanying, make a Psychic test. If the test is passed then roll D6 – on a 4+ the power is cancelled.

4 Psychic lash. The Sanctioned Psyker focuses his powers on nearby opponents, mentally ripping open arteries and puncturing organs. Make a Psychic test at the start of the Imperial Guard Assault phase. If successful, the power is in effect until the start of the next Imperial Guard Assault phase. Psychic lash can be used in a close combat when the Psyker would normally be able to make at least one attack. Instead of attacking normally, the Psyker gets D3 Attacks (with no bonuses for charging, additional weapons, etc) at Strength 3, with any wounds ignoring Armour saves (even if the target is not in base-to-base contact with the Psyker).

5 Machine curse. The Sanctioned Psyker presses his hands against an enemy vehicle and calls upon his powers to pronounce a curse on the machine spirits of his enemies.

This power is used in any Assault phase in place of normal attacks. Make the Psychic test at the start of the phase. If passed, the power is effective until the end of the same Assault phase. Make one close combat attack against the vehicle instead of any other attacks. If a hit is scored roll D6:

D6	Effect
1-3	No effect
4-5	Inflict glancing hit
6	Inflict penetrating hit

6 Lightning arc. Lightning leaps from the Psyker's hands, surrounding his body before being hurled at his enemies with a gesture.

This power is used in the Imperial Guard Shooting phase instead of firing a normal weapon and requires a successful Psychic test.

Lightning Arc – Range 24"; Strength 3; AP 6; Heavy D6.

☠ 0-5 COMMISSARS ☠

	Pts/Model	WS	BS	S	T	W	I	A	Ld	Sv
Commissar	40	4	4	3	3	2	4	2	10	5+

Number/squad: You may include up to five Commissars in your army. These do not count as one of your HQ choices and may be taken in addition to your usual allocation of HQ units in a mission. Each Commissar must join a separate unit in the army as described in the Advisors rule.

Weapons: Laspistol and close combat weapon.

Options: Commissars have access to the Imperial Guard Armoury and may select 'Officer only' items.

Transport: If the Officer they are attached to has a transport Chimera then the Commissar may also travel in it.

SPECIAL RULES

Advisors: See the sidebar on page 40.

It's For Your Own Good!: If a Sanctioned Psyker is attached to a unit which contains a Commissar and suffers a Perils of the Warp attack while using a psychic power, the Commissar will immediately execute him to prevent him being possessed. Remove the Psyker model as a casualty. The power he was attempting to use does not work.

Summary Execution: Commissars are tasked with ensuring unwavering dedication to the Imperial Creed and are utterly intolerant of backsliders. If a unit with a Commissar fails a Morale check for any reason, the Commissar will summarily execute the Officer or Sergeant leading the squad. This happens automatically – remove the executed model as a casualty. If he had a Trademark item, no Morale test is required in this case. The unit in question is then assumed to have passed the Morale test after all and continues to fight under the leadership of the Commissar.

The knowledge that a Commissar is looking over his shoulder for the slightest lapse focuses the mind of the Officer or Sergeant they are attached to considerably. The presence of a Commissar in a unit will therefore add +1 to the Leadership characteristic of the Officer or Sergeant commanding the unit for tests affecting the unit.

Rigid adherents to the Imperial Creed, Commissars are ruthless, fearless individuals whose dedication to the service of the Emperor overrides any compassion or mercy for the men they must sometimes lead in battle. Universally feared by those around them, Commissars have the power to execute any troopers (or officers) found wanting.

☠ 0-5 PRIESTS ☠

	Pts/Model	WS	BS	S	T	W	I	A	Ld	Sv
Priest	40	3	3	3	3	2	4	2	8	-

Number/squad: These do not count as one of your HQ choices and may be taken in addition to your usual allocation of HQ units in a mission. Each Priest must be attached to a unit as described in the Advisors special rule.

Weapons: Close combat weapon.

Options: Priests have access to the Imperial Guard Armoury. They may not select 'Officer only' items.

SPECIAL RULES

Advisors: See sidebar on page 40.

Fanatical: A Priest and the unit he is assigned to may re-roll any failed to hit rolls once in the turn they charge while the Priest lives.

Righteous Fury: Such is the rage imbued by a Priest's oratory that a unit including one <u>must</u> charge in the Assault phase if there are enemy in reach. In addition, such is their state of agitation that they always count as moving even if the models are stationary, so would be unable to fire heavy weapons.

Members of the Ecclesiarchy accompany many Imperial Guard regiments into battle. They ensure that the troops are sufficiently motivated to do their duty without fear, as well as fighting fanatically themselves.

ELITES

Guardsmen who survive long enough become experts at moving covertly through all forms of terrain and are extremely adept in close-range firefights. These grizzled survivors function best when allowed a certain amount of free reign, and they provide valuable experience in battlefield operations.

✠ 0-1 HARDENED VETERANS ✠

	Pts/Model	WS	BS	S	T	W	I	A	Ld	Sv
Veteran	8	3	4	3	3	1	3	1	8	5+
Veteran Sergeant	13	3	4	3	3	1	3	2	8	5+

Number/squad: Veteran Sergeant and between four and nine Veterans.

Weapons: Each model may be armed with either a lasgun OR a shotgun OR a laspistol and close combat weapon.

Options: Two Veterans may form a single heavy weapon crew. A heavy weapon crew must be armed with one of the weapons from the following list:

• lascannon at +25 pts; autocannon at +15 pts; mortar at +10 pts; heavy bolter at +10 pts; missile launcher at +15 pts.

Up to 3 Veterans not acting as heavy weapon crew may be armed with one of the special weapons from the following list:

• meltagun at +10 pts; plasma gun at +10 pts; grenade launcher at +8 pts; flamer at +6 pts.

Any Veteran not acting as heavy weapon crew or using a special weapon may be equipped with a vox-caster at +5 pts.

The entire squad can be equipped with frag grenades at +1 pt per model and/or krak grenades at +2 pts per model.

Character: The Hardened Veteran Sergeant has access to the Imperial Guard Armoury and may select 'Officer only' items.

Transport: The squad may be mounted in a Chimera transport vehicle at +70 pts. See the Chimera transport entry on page 45 for more details.

SPECIAL RULE
Infiltrators: If not equipped with a transport vehicle Veterans may be able to use their experience to take up an advanced position. They may therefore use the Infiltrators rule if it is permitted for the mission being used. If it is not permitted then they must set up with the rest of the army.

The huge strength and durability of Ogryns makes them perfect soldiers for the Imperial Guard. They require almost no training, although can only make use of the simplest of weapons. A select few may even have a glimmer of initiative which makes them prime candidates for augmetic surgery to boost their brain-power to the point where they can become an Ogryn Sergeant or Bone 'ead.

✠ OGRYNS ✠

	Pts/Model	WS	BS	S	T	W	I	A	Ld	Sv
Ogryn	25	4	3	5(6)	4	3	3	2	8	5+
Ogryn Bone 'ead	+10	4	3	5(6)	4	3	3	3	9	5+

Number/squad: The squad consists of between three and ten Ogryns.

Weapons: Ripper gun and frag grenades.

Character: One Ogryn may be upgraded to an Ogryn Bone 'ead at +10 pts. These Ogryns have their intellect boosted to enable them to understand more complex orders. A Bone'ead has access to the Imperial Guard Armoury, although he is not an Officer.

Transport: The squad may be mounted in a Chimera transport vehicle at +70 pts. See the Chimera transport entry on page 45 for more details.

SPECIAL RULES
Ogryn-proof: Ogryns will quickly break most guns by being over-enthusiastic with them in close combat. The ripper gun is built to be totally Ogryn-proof, however, and if used in close combat will add +1 to the Ogryn's Strength – such a solid lump of metal swung two-handed makes for an excellent club! This has already been included in the profile above.

"It's Dark in Dere!": Ogryns hate confined spaces and this can make it very difficult to get them into a Chimera. Because of this, an Ogryn squad will only embark if there is an Officer or a Commissar within 12" of at least one model in the unit when they embark. Ogryns can start mounted in a Chimera without an Officer or a Commissar being nearby (it's assumed they were convinced to enter the vehicle earlier on) and may disembark freely at any time. This rule does not apply if the unit is led by an Ogryn Bone'ead.

Bulky: Ogryns are bulky creatures and each one takes up two spaces in a transport vehicle.

✠ STORM TROOPERS ✠

	Pts/Model	WS	BS	S	T	W	I	A	Ld	Sv
Storm Trooper	10	3	4	3	3	1	3	1	8	4+
Storm Trooper Sergeant	10	3	4	3	3	1	3	1	8	4+
Veteran Sergeant	+6	3	4	3	3	1	3	2	8	4+

Number/squad: Sergeant and between four and nine Storm Troopers.

Weapons: The Sergeant carries a hellpistol and close combat weapon. The Storm Troopers have hellguns with targeters. All Storm Troopers have frag and krak grenades.

Options: Up to two Storm Troopers may be armed with one of the following special weapons:
• meltagun at +10 pts; plasma gun at +10 pts; flamer at +6 pts; grenade launcher at +8 pts. Storm Trooper squads may have meltabombs at +4 pts per model.
A Storm Trooper not armed with a special weapon may be upgraded to a Vox-operator at +5 pts.

Character: The Sergeant may be upgraded to be a Veteran Sergeant at +6 pts. A Veteran Sergeant has access to the Imperial Guard Armoury.

Transport: The squad may be mounted in a Chimera transport vehicle at +70 pts. See the Chimera transport entry on page 45 for more details.

SPECIAL RULES

Infiltrate/Deep Strike: Storm Trooper squads without a transport vehicle may either Infiltrate at +1 pt per model and/or Deep Strike at +1 pt per model, if the mission permits.

Storm Troopers are trained by the Schola Progenium to perform covert operations and spearhead assaults. The special treatment and elite status given to Storm Troopers causes a certain amount of rancour amongst regular Guardsmen and has earned them a variety of colourful and insulting nicknames, such as 'Glory Boys' and 'Big Toy Soldiers'.

✠ 0-1 RATLING SQUAD ✠

	Pts/Model	WS	BS	S	T	W	I	A	Ld	Sv
Ratling	11	2	4	2	2	1	4	1	6	5+

Number/squad: The squad consists between three and ten Ratlings.

Weapons: Sniper rifle.

SPECIAL RULES

Infiltrators: Ratlings may use the Infiltrators rule if it is permitted for the mission being used. If it is not permitted then the Ratlings must set up with the rest of the army.

Go to Ground: Ratlings have a strong sense of self-preservation. When in cover they get a +1 bonus to their Cover saving throws. Additionally, if required to take a Morale test for suffering 25% shooting casualties and are in cover, they may opt to be Pinned (as if they had failed a Pinning test from an Ordnance barrage) instead of taking the test.

Though unsuited for many battlefield roles, Ratlings make excellent snipers, a position that more often than not doesn't involve actual combat. Often the butt of soldier's jokes, more than one unit has had cause to be grateful for the covering fire of a unit of Ratling snipers.

✠ 0-1 TECHPRIEST ENGINSEERS ✠

	Pts/Model	WS	BS	S	T	W	I	A	Ld	Sv
Enginseer	45	3	3	3	3	1	3	1	8	3+

Number/squad: Up to two Techpriest Enginseers can be included in an army, and will count as a single Elite choice. They are deployed as a single unit but do not need to be placed together and operate independently during the game.

Weapons: Laspistol and power weapon (normally an axe), servo-arm.

Options: Techpriest Enginseers have access to the Imperial Guard Armoury. Servitors do not count towards the Enginseer's wargear limit.

Transport: A Techpriest Enginseer may be mounted in a Chimera transport vehicle at +70 pts. See the Chimera Transport entry on page 45 for more details.

Character: If on his own, a Techpriest Enginseer is an independent character. If accompanied by Servitors (see Wargear), he must remain in unit coherency with them and command them. If the Servitors are wiped out, the Techpriest Enginseer becomes an independent character.

SPECIAL RULES

Blessing of the Machine-God: A Techpriest Enginseer who starts the turn in contact with a damaged vehicle may attempt to make a repair. If the vehicle is immobilised or has a weapon destroyed, one of these defects (chosen by the Techpriest) is fixed on a roll of 6+. The Techpriest Enginseer gets +1 for each Technical Servitor accompanying him.

Privy to the mystical secrets of the engine-spirits of vehicles, the presence of an Enginseer is vital for a regiment's armoured units to function effectively. Either alone or aided by lobotomised servitors, they can often effect battlefield repairs to damaged vehicles.

TROOPS

The Infantry Platoon is the backbone of the Imperial Guard and is composed of a Command squad and two or more Infantry squads. This is the most common fighting unit of the Imperial Guard and, though its primary strength is its manpower, it is equipped with a wide range of powerful heavy weapons.

⬆ INFANTRY PLATOON ⬆

An Infantry Platoon consists of a Command Squad – a Junior Officer and his attendant staff, bought from the Command Squad entry on page 38 – and from 2 to 5 Infantry squads.

Each Platoon counts as a single Troops choice on the Force Organisation chart when deploying, and is rolled for collectively when rolling for reserves. Otherwise they function as independent units.

2-5 INFANTRY SQUADS . . . . .60 pts + weapons + upgrades

	Pts/Model	WS	BS	S	T	W	I	A	Ld	Sv
Guardsman	–	3	3	3	3	1	3	1	7	5+
Sergeant	–	3	3	3	3	1	3	1	7	5+
Veteran Sergeant	+6	3	3	3	3	1	3	2	8	5+

Number/squad: One Sergeant and nine Guardsmen.

Weapons: Sergeant may have laspistol and close combat weapon OR a shotgun OR a lasgun. Guardsmen have lasguns.

Options: Two Guardsmen may form a single heavy weapon crew. A heavy weapon crew must be armed with one of the weapons from the following list: missile launcher at +15 pts; lascannon at +25 pts; autocannon at +15 pts; mortar at +10 pts; heavy bolter at +10 pts.

One Guardsman not acting as heavy weapon crew may be armed with one of the special weapons from the following list: meltagun at +10 pts; plasma gun at +10 pts; grenade launcher at +8 pts; flamer at +6 pts.

Any Guardsman not acting as part of a heavy weapon crew or using a special weapon may be equipped with a vox-caster for +5 pts.

The entire squad can be equipped with frag grenades at +1 pt per model and/or krak grenades at +2 pts per model.

Character: The Sergeant may be upgraded to be a Veteran Sergeant at +6 pts. A Veteran Sergeant has access to the Imperial Guard Armoury.

Transport: None.

SPECIAL RULES

Remnants: Normally when a Platoon suffers casualties, depleted squads are merged to remain at full strength. There may be troops left over from this process, so each Platoon with at least two full squads (not counting HQ squads) may include a further squad at less than maximum strength. It will consist of a Sergeant and between four and eight Guardsmen at +6 pts each. They may not include a heavy weapon team but may include all other options.

↑ CONSCRIPT INFANTRY PLATOON ↑

	Pts/Model	WS	BS	S	T	W	I	A	Ld	Sv
Conscript	4	2	2	3	3	1	3	1	5	5+

A Conscript Platoon consists of between two and five squads. Each squad in the platoon will be made up as follows:

Number/squad: Ten Conscripts.

Weapons: Conscripts have lasguns.

Options: Up to one Conscript per squad may be armed with a flamer at +9 pts or a grenade launcher at +12 pts. Up to two Conscripts per squad may form a heavy weapons team with a heavy bolter at +15 pts, a missile launcher at +20 pts or an autocannon at +20 pts.

CONSCRIPT PLATOON

A Conscript Platoon consists of 2 to 5 squads. These function as a single unit of 20 to 50 models which must maintain the normal 2" squad coherency.

Squad organisation is only used to determine how many special and heavy weapons may be used.

You may include up to one Conscript Platoon for each normal Infantry Platoon in your army.

↑ ARMOURED FIST SQUAD ↑

ARMOURED FIST SQUAD . . .60 pts + weapons + upgrades + transport

	Pts/Model	WS	BS	S	T	W	I	A	Ld	Sv
Guardsman	–	3	3	3	3	1	3	1	7	5+
Veteran Sergeant	+6	3	3	3	3	1	3	2	8	5+

Up to one Armoured Fist squad may be fielded for each Infantry Platoon (but not Conscript Platoon) present.

Number/squad: Sergeant and nine Guardsmen.

Weapons: The Sergeant may have a laspistol and close combat weapon OR a shotgun OR a lasgun. Guardsmen have lasguns.

Options: Two Guardsmen may form a single heavy weapon crew. A heavy weapon crew must be armed with one of the following weapons: lascannon at +25 pts, missile launcher at +15 pts, autocannon at +15 pts, mortar at +10 pts or heavy bolter at +10 pts.

One Guardsman not acting as heavy weapon crew may be armed with one of the following special weapons: meltagun at +10 pts; plasma gun at +10 pts; flamer at +6 pts; grenade launcher at +8 pts.

Any Guardsman not acting as part of a heavy weapon crew or using a special weapon may be equipped with a vox-caster at +5 pts.

The entire squad can be equipped with frag grenades at +1 pt per model and/or krak grenades at +2 pts per model.

Character: The Sergeant may be upgraded to be a Veteran Sergeant at +6 pts. A Veteran Sergeant has access to the Imperial Guard Armoury.

Transport: The squad **must** be mounted in a Chimera transport at +70 pts (see below).

CHIMERA TRANSPORT

	Pts	Front Armour	Side Armour	Rear Armour	BS
Chimera	70+wpns	12	10	10	3

Type: Tank.　　**Crew:** Imperial Guard.

Weapons: The Chimera must have one of the following turret weapons: multi-laser at +10 pts; heavy flamer at +10 pts; heavy bolter at +10 pts. It may also have a heavy flamer or heavy bolter mounted in its hull at +5 pts.

Transport: A Chimera can transport up to 12 models. Remember that Ogryns take up two spaces each. A Chimera is always selected as a transport upgrade for another unit and may only transport the unit it was bought for. Independent characters that join a unit with a Chimera may also travel in it.

Access Points: Passengers enter and exit via the access ramp at the back of the hull.

Fire Points: The Chimera is fitted with six hull lasguns which can only be used by the passengers. Additionally, one model may fire a weapon from the top hatch but this will make the Chimera count as an Open-topped vehicle for the purposes of resolving shooting attacks in the next enemy turn.

Amphibious: Chimeras treat all water features as clear terrain when they move.

The ubiquitous transport vehicle of the Imperial Guard, Chimeras are extremely durable and practical vehicles, capable of mounting an array of infantry support weapons. Over the millennia, it has proved its reliability time and time again and remains a potent symbol of the Imperial Guard.

FAST ATTACK

A Hellhound is a flamer tank based on a Chimera hull that uses its Inferno cannon to burn enemy troops from cover. The vast reserves of promethium tanks it carries in place of its troop-carrying capacity has resulted in thicker armour plating and a gleeful pyromania amongst those who crew them.

✖ HELLHOUND ✖

	Pts	Front Armour	Side Armour	Rear Armour	BS
Hellhound	115	12	12	10	3

Type: Tank.   **Crew:** Imperial Guard.

Weapons: Turret-mounted Inferno cannon and hull-mounted heavy bolter.

SPECIAL RULE
Inferno cannon. The Inferno cannon fires a lethal gout of flame over considerable distances. Its profile is as follows:

Range 24"	Strength 6	AP 4	Heavy 1, Template

When firing the inferno cannon, designate a target unit and place the normal flamer template so that it is at least partially over as many unit members as possible. The whole template must be in range and line of sight. Roll to hit once, using the Hellhound's BS. If you hit, then all models partially or wholly under the template are hit. If you miss, they are each hit on a roll of 4+.

Many primitive cultures retain the use of mounted infantry, and Imperial Guard Infantry Platoons have often benefited from the deployment of their brand of fast-moving support. Rough Riders can carry a variety of weapons, but the most famous is without doubt the explosive-tipped hunting lance.

✖ ROUGH RIDER SQUADRON ✖

	Pts/Model	WS	BS	S	T	W	I	A	Ld	Sv
Rough Rider	8	3	3	3	3	1	3	1	7	5+
Veteran Sergeant	+6	3	3	3	3	1	3	2	8	5+

Number/squad: Sergeant and between four and nine Rough Rider troopers.

Weapons: Laspistol and close combat weapon.

Options: The squadron can replace their laspistols or close combat weapons with hunting lances at +3 pts per model.

Any number of models without hunting lances may substitute a lasgun or shotgun for their laspistol at no extra cost.

Up to two troopers, without hunting lances, may be armed with one of the following special weapons:

• meltagun at +10 pts; plasma gun at +10 pts; flamer at +6 pts; grenade launcher at +8 pts.

The squadron may be equipped with krak grenades at +2 pts per model and/or meltabombs at +4 pts per model.

One Guardsman not using a special weapon may be equipped with a vox-caster at +5 pts.

Character: The Sergeant may be upgraded to be a Veteran Sergeant at +6 pts. A Veteran Sergeant has access to the Imperial Guard Armoury.

SPECIAL RULES
Cavalry: Rough Riders are Cavalry (see the Warhammer 40,000 rulebook for more details).

Hunting Lance: Rough Riders are sometimes issued with a long hunting lance tipped with a shaped explosive charge. They will automatically use the lance in the first close combat they fight in a game, after which it cannot be used again.

A model using a hunting lance cannot use an additional close combat weapon but adds +2 to its Strength and Initiative when charging. A model using a hunting lance ignores Armour saves.

Fleet of Hoof: Normally, Cavalry manoeuvre at the walk so that they can easily handle their weaponry, keep the horses fresh and maintain formation. When necessary, they can break into a trot or gallop. In the Shooting phase you may state that the unit is going to move rather than shoot. Roll a D6 – this is the distance the unit may move in the Shooting phase.

✖ SENTINEL SQUADRON ✖

	Pts	WS	BS	S	Front Armour	Side Armour	Rear Armour	I	A
Sentinel	35	3	3	5	10	10	10	3	1

Type: Walker, Open-topped.   **Crew:** One Guardsman.

Squadron: A squadron consists of between one and three Sentinels.

Weapons: Each Sentinel in a squadron must be armed in accordance with one of the following configurations. (A squadron may contain several different patterns):

- Catachan pattern – heavy flamer (+5 pts)
- Mars pattern – multi-laser (+10 pts);
- Cadian pattern – autocannon (+15 pts)
- Armageddon pattern – lascannon (+20 pts).

SPECIAL RULE

Scouts: Sentinels are used to scout ahead and are always in the vanguard of the army. To represent this, any Sentinels in the army may be deployed at the start of a battle, even in scenarios where they could not normally be deployed.

For example, if you were the defender in a Take & Hold mission then your Sentinels would set up at the start of battle instead of being placed in reserve with the rest of the Fast Attack units. If you are playing a scenario where you can only deploy a limited number of units then any Sentinels you deploy are not counted against the limit for the scenario.

In addition to this rule, after both sides have deployed, any Sentinels may make a 'free' move. The move happens before dice are rolled to determine who takes first turn. All of the normal movement rules apply.

Sentinels are ideal scouting vehicles, and their pilots are often forced to use their own initiative – qualities not always fostered in Imperial soldiers. Many of these pilots are highly individualistic and have a reputation as insubordinate mavericks. When not pressed into service as scouts, they are often used to harry the flanks of enemy formations or act as mobile anti-armour squadrons.

If the enemy comes on in a great horde, as Orks are wont to do, then try to direct them into a narrow defile or enclosed space, such that their numbers work against them. Crowded together those at the front will impede those behind, whilst the push from the rear will prevent those at the front from retreating or finding a better path.

The Tactica Imperium

HEAVY SUPPORT

A Heavy Weapons Platoon is where the greatest proportion of the regiment's most powerful weapons are gathered together. Composed of a Command squad and several Support squads, they are equipped with the heaviest man-portable weapons in the regiment and are invaluable in providing defence against enemy armoured vehicles and large alien creatures.

∧ HEAVY WEAPONS PLATOON ∧

A Heavy Weapons Platoon consists of a Command Squad – a Junior Officer and his attendant staff, bought from the Command Squad entry on page 38 – and from 1 to 3 Support squads.

Each Platoon counts as a single Heavy Support choice on the Force Organisation chart when deploying, and is rolled for collectively when rolling for reserves. Otherwise, they function as independent units.

1-3 SUPPORT SQUADS

A Heavy Weapons Platoon must have 1-3 Support units, chosen from the following units on pages 38: Anti-tank squad, Fire Support squad, Mortar squad.

⋀ LEMAN RUSS BATTLE TANK ⋀

	Pts	Front Armour	Side Armour	Rear Armour	BS
Leman Russ	140+wpns	14	12	10	3

Type: Tank.   **Crew:** Imperial Guard.

Weapons: A Leman Russ Battle Tank is armed with a turret-mounted battle cannon and must have one of the following hull-mounted weapons: a lascannon at +15 pts, or a heavy bolter at +5 pts.

Options: The Leman Russ Battle Tank may be upgraded with two side sponsons armed with either a pair of heavy bolters at +10 pts or a pair of heavy flamers at +10 pts.

The Leman Russ Battle Tank is the most commonly found tank in Imperial Guard regiments. It is a simple design and one that has stood the test of time better than most; its versatility and relative ease of construction make it the tank most often requested by Imperial officers to be attached to their infantry formations.

⋀ LEMAN RUSS DEMOLISHER ⋀

	Pts	Front Armour	Side Armour	Rear Armour	BS
Demolisher	150+wpns	14	13	11	3

Type: Tank.   **Crew:** Imperial Guard.

Weapons: A Leman Russ Demolisher is armed with a turret-mounted Demolisher cannon and must have one of the following hull-mounted weapons: a lascannon at +15 pts, or a heavy bolter at +5 pts.

Options: The Leman Russ Demolisher may be upgraded with two side sponsons armed with either a pair of multi-meltas at +30 pts, a pair of plasma cannons at +20 pts, a pair of heavy bolters at +10 pts, or a pair of heavy flamers at +10 pts.

The Demolisher is a variant of the Leman Russ optimised for destroying the best protected targets. Their superior rear armour, powerful sponson weapon options and incredibly destructive cannon make them as effective in difficult terrain as in open country. Because of this they are highly valued for close support by Imperial Guard infantry.

⋀ BASILISK ⋀

	Pts	Front Armour	Side Armour	Rear Armour	BS
Basilisk	100	12	10	10	3

Type: Tank, Open-topped.   **Crew:** Imperial Guard.

Weapons: A Basilisk is armed with an 'Earthshaker' artillery gun and a hull-mounted heavy bolter.

Options: Indirect fire (+25 pts).

SPECIAL RULE
Indirect Fire: The Earthshaker crew may be trained to fire their artillery gun indirectly at targets that it cannot draw a line of sight to. If fired in this way, the Earthshaker is treated as a barrage (ie, Guess range) weapon with a minimum range of 36" and a maximum range of 240".

A fearsome piece of artillery, the Basilisk is capable of elevating to angles that allow it to fire at targets out of its field of vision. Its powerful shells are capable of smashing apart both infantry and vehicles with ease and the shriek of its incoming shells is rightly feared by the enemies of the Emperor.

LORD CASTELLAN URSARKAR E. CREED

The boy who was to become Lord Castellan Ursarkar E. Creed of Cadia was found in the war-wracked ruins of Kasr Gallan by soldiers of the 8th Cadian Regiment. He would not speak of the horrors he had endured but his faith in the Emperor and his own will were already forged into a weapon of iron that he did not hesitate to use. Impressed by his courage and strength, the 8th Regiment adopted him and he was inducted into the Youth Army or Whiteshield corps, and it was here he met Jarran Kell. The brooding Creed and garrulous Kell forged a bond that was to last for the rest of their lives. Already Creed was a natural leader and was driven by a fanatical devotion to the Imperial cause. Soon, his Whiteshield platoon was hurled into the five-year Drussite Crusade, and by the time the Cadian army celebrated victory in the blaze of the xeno-pyres, Creed was a Captain of the Shock Troops and Kell his colour sergeant.

As an officer, Ursarkar Creed was demanding of his men and himself. His personal example earned him unconditional respect. In important matters, he maintained the discipline expected of a Cadian unit but knew when to turn a blind eye, a quality that displeased many a Commissar. Creed rarely had to repeat an order; instead he exuded an intensity that compelled obedience from all around him. His greatest strength though was his understanding of how a Cadian force should fight – not for him the unthinking exchange of lives so beloved of other Imperial Guard officers. Creed mixed resolute defence with blistering counter-attacks, proving himself as capable of leading an army as a platoon.

With Kell ever at his side, Creed fought throughout the Hrud migration of 983-5.M41 and was commander of the force that hunted down the Chaos Space Marine Lord Brule on Trecondal. His first action as a Lord General of Cadia saw him not only defeat, but annihilate the Ulthwé raid on Aurent in 992.M41. By now he was Cadia's most successful living commander, and only his lowly birth held his career in check.

In 999.M41, a murderous plot by the forces of the Great Enemy killed several members of the Cadian High Command. In times of such dire emergency there existed a special military rank, Lord Castellan of Cadia, bestowed for life or until the emergency was over. Returning to Cadia from his latest campaign, Creed was met with massive acclaim from the rank and file of the Cadian army. One by one his potential rivals stepped down in the interests of unity until the foundling boy was, by common consent, appointed Lord Castellan of Cadia. In the dark days that followed, he would need all his faith and all his skill.

Any Cadian army of at least 1,500 points may be led by Creed. He has always insisted that no officer should fear front-line duty and habitually lives up to his own words. His lifelong comrade, Sergeant Jarran Kell, always accompanies him to battle and is responsible for ensuring his survival. If the army Command Platoon has a Chimera transport then Creed and Kell may commandeer it for their own use (the original owners have to walk!). If so, this must be declared before deployment commences.

Ursarkar Creed and Jarran Kell are always used together although on the battlefield, both are independent characters and can separate and join different units as desired. Both must be used as listed, occupying a single HQ slot on the Force Organisation chart. The points cost listed is for both characters. Victory points are awarded on the basis of wounds inflicted on Creed only. No Victory points are scored for killing or wounding Kell.

URSARKAR CREED

	Points	WS	BS	S	T	W	I	A	Ld	Sv
Creed	125	4	4	3	3	3	4	3	10	4+

Wargear: Trademark item (pistols), refractor field, carapace armour, two matched hellpistols (fire as twin-linked hellpistol, count as additional close combat weapon in close combat).

SPECIAL RULES
Iron Discipline. See rules on page 56.

Master Strategist. Where there is a choice of mission based on strategy rating, an army containing Creed may always choose the mission. Similarly, they may either choose to win the dice roll for choice of table edge or request that the dice for the first turn be re-rolled.

> What do I ask of my officers? Merely that they do their duty with fire in their bellies and a prayer on their lips.
>
> Lord Castellan Ursarkar E. Creed

COLOUR SERGEANT JARRAN KELL

	Points	WS	BS	S	T	W	I	A	Ld	Sv
Kell	–	5	5	3	3	3	4	3	8	4+

Where Creed is silent and calculating, Kell is his voice, roaring and bombastic as only a colour sergeant can be. He has made keeping Creed alive his life's work and has the wounds to prove it. A fearsome fighter, his amplified voice drowns out the war cries of the enemy and ensures that Creed's orders are obeyed in the heat of battle. Although nominally a sergeant, Kell has all the privileges of being an Officer, including the Command special rule.

Wargear: Medallion Crimson, carapace armour, regimental banner, power fist, power sword. The regimental banner is that of the 8th Cadian Regiment, and counts as the one regimental banner allowed in the army.

SPECIAL RULES
Iron Discipline. See rules on page 56.

Bodyguard. If within 2" of Creed, then Kell may change places with him at the start of either player's Assault phase. He will then fight Creed's opponents and Creed will fight his (if any).

Ursarkar Creed directs the destruction of the Volscani Cataphracts at the Battle of Tyrok Fields

COMMISSAR YARRICK

"Heroes of Armageddon! You have withstood the evil savagery of the Orks, and they have nothing left for you to fear. So raise high the black banners of vengeance – now is our time."

Last transmission from Commissar Yarrick prior to departing with a Black Templars crusade to hunt down Ghazghkull Mag Uruk Thraka.

The name of Commissar Yarrick is known throughout the Imperium of Man, and his praises are sung across a thousand worlds. To the men of the Imperial Guard he is a hero, a deliverer who saved the world of Armageddon from the depredations of the Ork Warlord Ghazghkull Mag Uruk Thraka on not one, but two separate occasions.

It was during the Second War for Armageddon that Yarrick rose to fame. Though an old man, he led a masterful defence of the beleaguered Hades Hive, inspiring the battered defenders to prodigious acts of sacrifice. His defence stalled the Ork invasion and eventually led to the Imperium's glorious, though costly, victory.

In the wake of the Second War, Yarrick was commonly seen as having earned a peaceful retirement. But the commissar was haunted by the knowledge that Ghazghkull lived, and devoted the remainder of his years to hunting down the 'Beast of Armageddon'.

Fifty years later, Ghazghkull returned to Armageddon, initiating the Third War. Yarrick returned once more to oppose the Ork warlord, and this time took command of the entire world's armed forces. Millions lost their lives during the Third War for Armageddon, and the conflict soon degenerated into a gruelling war of attrition in which neither side could gain a clear advantage. Though Ghazghkull Mag Uruk Thraka himself was repulsed from the world, Yarrick vowed never to rest until he is made to pay for the death and destruction he has visited upon the worlds of the Imperium.

COMMISSAR YARRICK

	Points	WS	BS	S	T	W	I	A	Ld	Sv
Yarrick	146	5	4	3	3	3	4	3	10	4+

An Imperial Guard army of 2,000 points or more may include Commissar Yarrick. If you take him then he counts as one of the HQ choices for the army. He must be used exactly as described below, and may not be given any additional equipment.

Wargear: Master-crafted storm bolter, laspistol, carapace armour, force field, Bale Eye, battle claw (counts as a power fist), Medallion Crimson.

SPECIAL RULES

Force Field: Yarrick is protected by a special force field that reduces the energy of enemy attacks. Whenever he is hit, roll a D6 and deduct the number shown on the dice from the Strength of the attack. If reduced to 0 or less, the attack is stopped completely. The force field has no effect on attacks that don't use Strength to inflict damage.

Bale Eye: Yarrick's Bale Eye is a bionic implant that incorporates a laser. It can be fired once per Assault phase at Yarrick's normal Initiative, in addition to his base attacks. The attack automatically inflicts a Strength 4, AP - hit on a single model in base contact with him, chosen by the Imperial Guard player.

Independent Character: Commissar Yarrick is an independent character and follows all of the rules for characters in the Warhammer 40,000 rulebook.

Fearless: Yarrick is totally fearless and never has to take Morale or Pinning tests. He confers this ability to any unit he joins.

Leader: In addition to his rank of Commissar, Yarrick is a leader of men. The Advisors special rule does not apply to him – he is free to act independently or join any squad that does not already have an independent character attached. He will not carry out a Summary Execution (as any unit he joins becomes Fearless) but he will execute a Sanctioned Psyker subject to the It's For Your Own Good special rule.

COLONEL-COMMISSAR IBRAM GAUNT

"I am a Commissar. I am empowered to deliver justice wherever I see it lacking. I am empowered to punish cowardice. I am granted the gift of total authority to judge, in the name of the Emperor, on the field of combat."

Colonel-Commissar Ibram Gaunt, prior to the field execution of his uncle General Aldo Dercius

When the forest world of Tanith fell to a surprise attack by the vanguard of a Chaos fleet, the troops there were in no state to repel them. The forces mustered from the planet, intended for war in the Sabbat Worlds Crusade, were barely founded when a storm of destruction rained down upon their peaceful, arboreal world. Commissar Gaunt, entrusted with the command of the emergent Tanith regiments, was forced to make a decision that shaped his own destiny and that of the surviving troops. Evacuating as many of the soldiers as he could during the Chaos attack, Gaunt robbed the Tanith of a chance to fight and die with their homeworld. Two whole regiments were lost. The remaining men, alone and without a planet to call home, now call themselves 'Gaunt's Ghosts'.

Since that point and his subsequent promotion to Colonel-Commissar, Gaunt has slowly won the devotion and respect of the one surviving regiment, leading them through hellish theatres of war to glorious victory time and time again. Gaunt is a gifted commander who leads from the front line, and over the years he has won an unswerving devotion from the Tanith 1st (often known as the First & Only). He is feared in the upper echelons of the Imperial Guard as much as by his enemies on the battlefield, for in everything he does, Gaunt is unwavering, certain and resolute. His uncompromising code of honour and defiance of corruption in all its forms stands as an exemplary model of conduct to his troops and his peers alike.

of heroism in his men that all Tanith Imperial Guard models in that combat benefit from +1 Attack for that round only. This benefit includes Gaunt himself.

Camo-cloak: Gaunt's camo-cloak adds +1 to any Cover saves he is allowed (eg, a 5+ Cover save becomes a 4+ Cover save). He receives no Cover save when in the open.

Independent Character: Colonel-Commissar Gaunt is an independent character and follows all of the rules for characters in the Warhammer 40,000 rulebook.

Fearless: Gaunt is totally fearless and never has to take Morale or Pinning tests. He confers this ability to any unit he joins.

Leader: In addition to his rank of Colonel-Commissar, Gaunt is a leader of men. The Advisors special rule does not apply to him – he is free to act independently. He will not carry out a Summary Execution (as any unit he joins becomes Fearless) but he will execute a Sanctioned Psyker subject to the It's For Your Own Good! special rule. Furthermore, any Imperial Guard squad within 12" of Colonel-Commissar Gaunt may use his Leadership value for all Morale and Pinning tests.

COLONEL-COMMISSAR IBRAM GAUNT

	Pts	WS	BS	S	T	W	I	A	Ld	Sv
Gaunt	75	5	4	3(4)	3	3	4	3	10	5+

An Imperial Guard army of 1,500 points or more may include Colonel-Commissar Gaunt. If you take him then he counts as one of the HQ choices for the army. He must be used exactly as described below, and may not be given any additional equipment.

Wargear: Sword of Heironymo, bolt pistol, camo-cloak, frag & krak grenades.

SPECIAL RULES
Sword of Heironymo: This sword is a priceless heirloom and replaced his characteristic chainsword when it was gifted to Gaunt for his actions in the city of Vervunhive. It is a master-crafted power sword and hits at Strength 4 (this is included in the profile above). It also counts as a trademark item.

Front-liner: Commissar Gaunt has always led from the front, and will plunge into the thick of the fighting without hesitation. If there is an assault occurring within 12" of Gaunt at the start of the Imperial Guard player's turn and he is not in combat, he must immediately move toward the nearest combat in his Movement phase and assault the enemy models in that combat if at all possible. However, when Gaunt charges into an assault, he inspires such feats

COLONEL SCHAEFFER'S LAST CHANCERS

The Thirteenth Penal Legion is better known as Schaeffer's Last Chancers. Led by the fiercely uncompromising Colonel Schaeffer, the unit is the last stop for psychopaths, recidivists, thieves and other assorted scum otherwise destined for the firing squad. Schaeffer's ethos is simple; he will give the troops in his charge one chance to win the God-Emperor's forgiveness and in so doing save their souls. He will give them this chance by leading them into the most dangerous warzones to perform the most suicidal missions. Then, if they live, as his second-in-command Kage has continued to do, as much out of a desire to see Schaeffer dead as anything else, he will lead them into another potential death-trap.

Initially, Colonel Schaeffer might recruit thousands of bad characters but he will ensure that these are whittled down in battle until only the hard core remain before leading them on the mission they were really recruited for. It is rare for a Last Chancer to live for long so it is up to you to define exactly who YOUR Last Chancers are going to be. They might include the Veteran Sergeant who failed his 'Last Man Standing' test and ran off table in the last game or the squad that were standing around doing nothing when the enemy blew up the objective in the Sabotage mission. Whoever they are, the Colonel and Lieutenant Kage will lead them into hell, but probably not back.

The Last Chancers count as a HQ selection on the Force Organisation Chart. If more than 8 models are taken (including Schaeffer and Kage) they count as a Troops selection as well. If more than 16 models are taken they count as two Troops selections as well.

	Pts/Model	WS	BS	S	T	W	I	A	Ld	Sv
Schaeffer	75	5	4	3	3	3	4	3	9	4+
Kage	35	4	4	3	3	2	4	3	8	5+
Last Chancer	11	3	4	3	3	1	3	2	8	5+

Number/squad: Colonel Schaeffer, Lieutenant Kage and from 4 to 20 Last Chancers.

Weapons: Schaeffer has a power sword, plasma pistol and carapace armour. He also has bionics, the Macharian Cross and a Medallion Crimson.

Kage has a bolt pistol and close combat weapon.

The Last Chancers have a motley assortment of personal weapons, but in game terms each will have either a lasgun, a shotgun or a laspistol and close combat weapon.

All members of the unit have frag and krak grenades.

Options: Schaeffer and Kage must be used as described. Any number of Last Chancers can be upgraded to specialists at +5 points per model.

Each specialist may be armed with a special or heavy weapon from the list below, and may additionally select equipment from the Imperial Guard Armoury up to a maximum limit of 15 points each (this can include 'Officer only' items – some of the owners may not have noticed the kit is missing yet!). Weapon limits apply (no model may have more than two weapons of which only one can be two-handed) and weapons selected from the list below cannot be master-crafted.

For each model with a heavy weapon, there must be at least one more non-specialist charged with carrying the ammo. Each pair of models will form a heavy weapon team armed with one of the following: lascannon at +25 points, missile launcher at +15 points, autocannon at +15 points, heavy bolter at +10 points or mortar at +10 points.

Otherwise, specialists can carry a meltagun at +10 points, plasma gun at +10 points, flamer at +6 points, grenade launcher at +8 points, sniper rifle at +10 points or demolition charge at +10 points.

Any specialist not acting as heavy weapon team or using a special weapon may be equipped with a vox-caster at +5 points.

Any specialist not acting as heavy weapon team or using a special weapon may be upgraded to a Psyker for +5 points. His profile remains the same but he has a randomly determined power from the Sanctioned Psyker table.

Character: Schaeffer and Kage are independent characters. They must remain within 2" of the sub-unit they are each allocated to (see Sub-Units below) at all times and may not leave it. If it is wiped out each reverts to being an independent character.

Transport: Any sub-unit may be mounted in a Chimera transport at +70 points; see the Chimera entry on page 49 for more details.

SPECIAL RULES

Sub-Units. At the start of any game you can break the Last Chancers, including Kage and Schaeffer, into a maximum of five sub-units. Each can consist of as few as one model. How you do this is up to you but you cannot have more than five units.

Members of the same heavy weapon team must be in the same sub-unit and no sub-unit may have more than one demolition charge.

Doctrines. The Last Chancers come from a variety of units and cannot be upgraded with any Doctrines.

Harsh Discipline. While the Colonel is alive all sub-units will automatically pass any Morale, Leadership or Pinning tests they have to make.

Crazy. Lieutenant Kage is a nasty piece of work with a mind no one wants to understand too closely. When attacking a sentry, the alarm is only raised on a 6, as Kage is a very proficient back-stabber. Also he gets premonitions – sometimes they just encourage him to do bad things, but other times they warn him of danger. Treat his 5+ save as Invulnerable.

Infiltrate. Any sub-unit not mounted in a Chimera may infiltrate if the mission permits it.

Deep Strike. Any sub-unit not mounted in a Chimera may start the game in reserve and arrive by Deep Strike if the mission permits it. This represents them dropping in by grav-chute.

REGIMENTAL DOCTRINES

Although there is a great deal of standardisation within the Imperial Guard there are many regimental traditions and skills peculiar to their homeworld that make many regiments slightly different. It is this universal diversity that produces the myriad of different colours and flavours of Imperial Guard troopers and regiments, and to allow players to use the army list to produce their own specialised regiments we have introduced a system called 'Doctrines'.

Doctrines are variations in training and organisation that have an effect on the way a regiment fights. They are only relevant if you want your army to represent a particular regiment with minimal external support. Using the full list without Doctrines is always a valid option and is perfectly representative of any number of regiments from Cadian Shock Troops to Catachan Jungle Fighters to Drookian Fen Troopers.

If you want to use Doctrines, the procedure is quite simple:

- You are allowed **five** Doctrine points to define your regiment's specialisations. You do not have to use all five but there is no benefit in using less.

- All unit entries shown under the Restricted Troops heading below are unavailable, unless you 'buy back' these troops with some of your five Doctrine points.

- Doctrine points can also be expended to give the regiment a different alternate organisational structure, skills, drills and special equipment.

- Purchase of some Doctrines may increase the basic costs associated with the various troop types.

Unless specifically stated, Doctrines cannot be taken more than once and never 'stack' in any way. Doctrines cannot be used by troops who are allied to the Imperial Guard army, such as indentured Imperial Guard in an inquisitorial allied contingent.

On pages 58 to 61 we have included some famous regiments and the Doctrines which represent their typical organisation in battle. You will notice that the some regiments may have more than five Doctrines; this is a reflection of their glorious history. In practice five Doctrines is plenty to give a regiment a distinctive slant. Again, there is no requirement to use the Doctrines rules for fielding any particular regiment.

Doctrines are spread across four broad categories: *Restricted Troops, Alternate Regimental Organisation, Skills and Drills* and *Special Equipment.*

Guard Infantry
In several of the following Doctrine descriptions, the term Guard Infantry unit is used. In this context, the definition includes any command squad along with its Officer and any attached advisors, Anti-tank squads, Fire Support squads, Special Weapons squads (if the regiment may use them), Mortar squads, Hardened Veteran squads, normal Infantry Platoon squads and Armoured Fist squads.

RESTRICTED TROOPS

The first category of Doctrines allows the regiment to select Restricted Troops. If you do not select a troop type as a Restricted Unit Doctrine then you may not include them in your army. Each of the entries listed on the right that you

wish to use will take up one of your available Doctrine choices. Selecting any of these Doctrines will allow you to select the army list entry specified. The choices made say a lot about the world on which your regiment was recruited: Ratling and Ogryn squads imply a tolerance for abhumans that is not that commonplace as well as the existence of a community of these creatures on or close to the regiment's home world, Enginseers are representative of close ties to the Adeptus Mechanicus, Conscript platoons denote a heavily populated or highly militarised world, and so on.

For example, in the Death Korps of Krieg, infantry regiments are often closely supported by the Death Riders, a local form of Rough Rider mounted on cybernetically-altered steeds. If you wanted to use Doctrines to define the Death Korps then you would start by selecting the Rough Rider Doctrine to allow you to field units of Death Riders.

This Doctrine may be taken more than once to allow access to several Restricted troop types.

RESTRICTED TROOPS	
Priests	*You will note that there are ten restricted troop types on the list so with only five Doctrines at your disposal a regiment designed using Doctrines will always be slightly more restrictive than armies designed using the full list. This is counterbalanced by the alternate organisations and the skills and drills listed below which can only be used by a regiment designed using the Doctrines system.*
Techpriest Enginseers	
Sanctioned Psykers	
Storm Trooper squads	
Ratling squads	
Ogryn squads	
Special Weapon squads	
Conscript Platoons	
Rough Rider squadrons	
Heavy Weapon platoons	

ALTERNATE REGIMENTAL ORGANISATIONS

The main Imperial Guard list assumes that the force being used is a combined one pulled together from units in the theatre of operations and based around a standard infantry regiment. There are many different kinds of regiment in the Imperial Guard, however, and by selecting any of these Doctrines you will change the nature of your regiment quite fundamentally.

DROP TROOPS

This regiment comes from a world where grav-chute use is commonplace and has been trained in their use for dropping into combat. Any Guard Infantry unit (without a Chimera transport) or Sentinel squadron may Deep Strike if the mission permits. Other units must deploy conventionally. (As an aside, this Doctrine could be rationalised by stating the troops are emerging from Imperial tunnelling vehicles although this would be much rarer.)

May not be combined with Special Equipment: Warrior Weapons.

GRENADIERS

The regiment comes from a world where the best Imperial Guard recruits are combined into elite formations and receive superior training that is the equal of that provided to Storm Troopers.

The regiment may include 0-3 Storm Trooper squads as Troops. These Storm Troopers may not Deep Strike or Infiltrate.

May not be combined with Special Equipment:Warrior Weapons.

MECHANISED

The regiment is uniformly mounted in Chimera transport vehicles and specialises in mobile warfare. All Guard Infantry units must take a Chimera transport whether they normally have the option or not.

May not be combined with Special Equipment: Warrior Weapons or Light Infantry.

SKILLS AND DRILLS

These abilities represent techniques developed initially by veteran troops, which are then incorporated into the regiment's regular training drills to ensure successive generations of troops learn from their predecessors. Additionally some abilities are a consequence of the homeworld on which the regiment was raised.

DIE-HARDS

The regiment is so firmly indoctrinated into the Imperial faith and its own martial traditions that they will stand against overwhelming odds. Any Imperial Guard Infantry unit or Rough Rider squadron may be given this ability at a cost of +5 points. Die-hard squads do not count negative Morale modifiers for being outnumbered in close combat.

May not be combined with Special Equipment: Chem-inhalers.

IRON DISCIPLINE

On many worlds of the Imperium, nobles are raised from birth to be officers. They have an air of confidence and authority that keeps their troops fighting to the last man. Any unit using the Leadership characteristic of an Officer or Senior Officer with the Iron Discipline ability, for a Morale or Pinning test ignores the -1 modifier for being under half strength and may regroup even if below half strength. Any Officers can be given this ability for +5 points each.

May not be combined with Special Equipment: Chem-inhalers.

INDEPENDENT COMMISSARS

Rather than using Commissars as Advisors, some regiments give them a free hand to roam the battlefield. These Commissars act as independent characters with 1-3 forming a single Elite choice. They are deployed as a single unit but do not need to be placed together and operate independently during the game. Commissars cannot be used both as an Elite and an HQ choice. Every Commissar selected costs +10 points.

CLOSE ORDER DRILL

Members of the regiment are thoroughly drilled in fighting in dense formations where they can present a hedge of blades, bayonets and clubbed lasguns at the enemy. This drill is only used by units in standard Infantry Platoons and Conscript Infantry Platoons. To perform close order drill all the models in the unit must be in base to base contact.

While in close order, all models in the unit have +1 Leadership and +1 Initiative. Note that the Leadership bonus only applies when the unit's own Leadership is used (rather than that of an Officer within 12" for example).

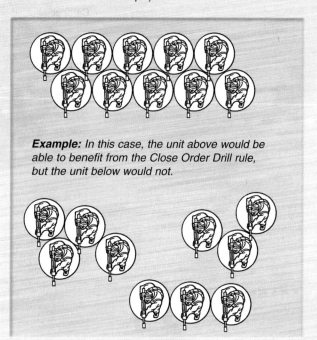

Example: In this case, the unit above would be able to benefit from the Close Order Drill rule, but the unit below would not.

HARDENED FIGHTERS

The regiment is recruited from particularly violent societies and backgrounds, and are particularly adept hand-to-hand combatants. Hardened Fighters add 1 to their WS. Sentinels additionally gain +1 Attack as their machine is fitted with chainsaw blades, rams and other accoutrements. This Doctrine is available to any Guard Infantry squad for +15 points per unit or to a Sentinel squadron at a cost of +10 points per Sentinel.

JUNGLE FIGHTERS

The regiment's members are recruited from a world with extensive thick forest or jungle. Any Guard Infantry unit can be upgraded to Jungle Fighters at +10 points per unit. Jungle Fighters gain the following benefits:

- Can see 12" through forest or jungle terrain;
- Receive a 4+ Cover save when in forest or jungle terrain;
- Move at full speed in forest or jungle terrain;
- May Infiltrate if the mission permits and they deploy in woods or jungle;
- Any Infantry squad normally able to include a heavy weapon team but not including one can upgrade a single Guardsman to carry a heavy flamer at +15 points instead;
- Jungle fighter units may never include lascannons.

This specialisation will lead a regiment to abandon bulky flak armour for a simple flak vest instead. All units taking this Doctrine reduce their Armour save from 5+ to 6+.

May not be combined with Special Equipment: Cameleoline or Special Equipment: Carapace Armour.

LIGHT INFANTRY

The regiment is renowned for its stealth. This Doctrine is available to any Guard Infantry unit without a transport vehicle at +10 points per unit. A unit with this ability:

- Rolls an additional dice when determining how far they can move through difficult terrain;
- May infiltrate if the mission permits;
- May, if they are a normal Infantry Platoon squad that could include a heavy weapon team but chooses not to, upgrade a single Guardsman's lasgun to a sniper rifle at +5 points.

May not be combined with Special Equipment: Carapace Armour or Mechanised.

SHARPSHOOTERS

Sometimes war has been a way of life for successive generations of the regiment, and consequently they are formidable marksmen, having undergone military training from an early age. Any Guard Infantry model with a BS of 3 may make a single re-roll of a shooting to hit roll of 1. The Sharpshooter ability has no effect when firing plasma weapons (which few men survive using long enough to master) or sniper rifles (where the slightest inaccuracy ruins the shot). This ability costs 10 points for a unit and can be applied to any Guard Infantry unit with at least one BS3 model.

XENO-FIGHTERS

After numerous wars, the regiment has learnt how to combat particular types of xeno. The permissible types are Orks, Eldar (including Dark Eldar), and Tyranids. Any Guard Infantry unit or Sentinel squadron may be upgraded to Xeno-fighters (you must specify the type of xeno) at a cost of +5 points per infantry unit or Sentinel.

When in close combat with any enemy of that race with a WS attribute, Xenos-fighters hit on 3+ regardless of respective Weapon Skill values.

This advantage does not apply if the enemy has the independent character, Tyranid Monstrous Creature or Monstrous Creature rule. Too few men survive their first confrontation with such dangerous xenos to build real expertise.

The type of xenos species the regiment specialises in fighting must be apparent from trophies such as helmets/heads suspended from belts and vehicles or special standards. Some form of representation of the race in question on the regiment's members is mandatory for this Doctrine. It is absolutely unacceptable to simply switch specialisation to match your next opponent.

VETERANS

The regiment has been in service for several campaigns and includes a far higher ratio of Veterans than normal. The normal 0-1 limit on Hardened Veteran units does not apply to this regiment.

SPECIAL EQUIPMENT

Some regiments are equipped with a piece of non-standard equipment that is a speciality of their world or follow a training regime substantially different from that of most Guard regiments. Whatever the reason the regiment has a special trait. The Tanith 1st's cameleoline camo-cloaks for example come into this category.

The items below are examples that you can use initially; other examples will be introduced in the future. This Doctrine can be taken more than once with each selection granting access to a different special piece of equipment. It is therefore possible to have troops with cameleoline and carapace armour, this could be rationalised as armour with 'stealth' qualities.

If this Doctrine is taken then each special piece of equipment must be applied to every available model so if you choose cameleoline then every model that can have it, must have it. However if a Doctrine can be applied to Rough Riders you can choose to apply it to Rough Riders only.

SPECIAL EQUIPMENT

Chem-inhaler. Some undisciplined units have altered the gasses in their rebreathers to include narcotics such as 'slaught and Kalma. The effect is to make them even more indifferent to danger and loss. They will always test Morale, Leadership or Pinning with no negative modifiers. If they fail a Morale check for 25% shooting casualties, they will be pinned rather than falling back. Costs +10 points per unit.

May not be combined with Iron Discipline or Die-hards.

Cameleoline. Some units are able to use the rare cameleoline material in their uniforms or as cloaks. Cameleoline automatically blends in with the surrounding terrain making the wearer much harder to spot. Any Guard Infantry unit with cameleoline camouflage adds 1 to any Cover save they are already allowed. Costs +10 points per unit.

May not be combined with Jungle Fighters.

Carapace armour. Guard Infantry units and Rough Rider squadrons upgrade their normal flak armour with carapace armour at +20 points per unit. This means that their Armour save will change from 5+ to 4+. Sometimes this will be conventional carapace armour, alternatively it may be bulky feral platemail.

May not be combined with Light Infantry or Jungle Fighters.

Cyber-enhancement. The regiment is recruited from a world where extensive use is made of cybernetic enhancement and replacement. This is most common in the servants of the Adeptus Mechanicus. Guard Infantry unit or Rough Rider units are cybernetically augmented at +20 points for the unit. Such a unit has an Invulnerable save of 6 representing enemy attacks bouncing off their augmentations.

Warrior Weapons. The regiment is recruited from primitive warriors. Any model normally armed with a lasgun that does not have access to the Armoury replaces it with a laspistol and close combat weapon or a pair of close combat weapons at a cost of +2 points per model.

May not be selected with Drop Troops, Mechanised or Grenadiers.

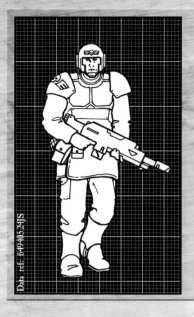

CADIAN SHOCK TROOPS

Cadia has always been a fortress world, charged with guarding the entrance to the Eye of Terror. Its population are all destined for a military life; the birth rate and recruitment rate are synonymous. Cadian Regiments are highly disciplined, make excellent shots and use elite shock troops to lead their attacks. Such is the reputation of the Cadian Shock Troops that many other regiments mimic their appearance, although their doctrines may differ.

Preferred special weapon: Grenade Launcher
Preferred heavy weapon: Autocannon

- Grenadiers
- Sanctioned Psykers
- Special Weapon squads
- Storm Trooper squads
- Iron Discipline
- Sharpshooters
- Conscript platoons

There is only the Emperor and he is our shield and protector

Data ref: 649405.24JS

VALHALLAN ICE WARRIORS

From their earliest victories against the Orks on Valhalla, the Ice Warriors have a reputation for stoicism and dedication to the Emperor. Regiments raised in the frozen hive cities of Valhalla have a formidable reputation for unwavering courage when on the defensive. Normally the only way to capture ground held by Valhallans is by wiping them out. When attacking, they combine massed artillery barrages with infantry wave assaults.

Preferred special weapon: Flamer
Preferred heavy weapon: Mortar

- Heavy Weapon platoons
- Priests
- Conscript platoons
- Xeno-fighters: Orks
- Close Order Drill
- Veterans

Data ref: 928x/4

TALLARN DESERT RAIDERS

The Tallarn are mobile guerrilla fighters, evasive and opportunistic. They are especially well-known for their hard-fighting Sentinel squadrons and are masters of hit-and-run warfare. Tallarn are all accomplished riders, often they will use riding mounts to move from battle to battle, dismounting only when they are close to the enemy and wish to employ stealth. Once the enemy are sighted the Tallarn will stalk them relying on their practiced marksmanship and lighting-quick curved knives to achieve victory.

Preferred special weapon: Plasma gun
Preferred heavy weapon: Missile Launcher

- Priests
- Hardened Fighters
- Rough Rider squadrons
- Light Infantry
- Sharpshooters

The blood of martyrs is the seed of the Imperium. 4

Data ref: JW-02/07

MORDIAN IRON GUARD

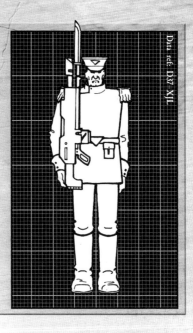

The Mordian Iron Guard are superbly drilled and accoutred soldiers from a world bathed in perpetual night and cursed with the attentions of Chaos. In battle the Iron Guard present a solid wall of brightly-uniformed, perfectly formed troops to the enemy, cutting them down with precisely timed volleys from behind a hedge of bayonet points. Some enemies of the Emperor have been misled by the Mordians' elaborate and ornate uniforms to believe they were facing amateurs, only to find the bright uniforms contain tough, determined soldiers.

Preferred special weapon: Grenade Launcher
Preferred heavy weapon: Lascannon

- Sanctioned Psykers
- Ratling squads
- Heavy Weapon platoons
- Sharpshooters
- Close Order Drill
- Die-hards

Thought for the day: Hope is the first step on the road to disappointment.

ARMAGEDDON STEEL LEGIONS

The Steel Legions are renowned for their skill in opposing the Orks on the great ash wastes of their native world. Fully mobile in their Chimera transports, they are able to launch rapid attacks in which the Chimeras overrun the enemy lines before the Steel Legion infantry dismount to finish them off. Fighting in proximity to the great Hives of Armageddon, the Steel Legions are sometimes supported by hive militia conscripts eager to join their ranks.

Preferred special weapon: Grenade Launcher
Preferred heavy weapon: Missile Launcher

- Mechanised
- Storm Trooper squads
- Xeno-fighters: Orks
- Ratling squads
- Conscript platoons

TANITH FIRST & ONLY

The Tanith homeworld was destroyed shortly after the regiment was founded, leaving them orphaned. They carry with them the wilderness skills learnt on their homeworld that make them superb light infantry. Led by the inspirational Colonel-Commissar Gaunt, and drawing new recruits from the worlds they fight to defend, their reputation continues to grow with each victory.

Preferred special weapon: Flamer
Preferred heavy weapon: Missile Launcher

- Light Infantry
- Priests
- Sharpshooters
- Veterans
- Hardened Fighters
- Independent Commissars
- Special Equipment: Cameleoline

Data access restricted –
Ordo Malleus auth. ref. X6-975-826-109

Only the awkward question; only the foolish ask twice

CATACHAN JUNGLE FIGHTERS

The planet Catachan is a deathworld in which the climate, animal life and plant life is all inimical to humanity. On Catachan, daily survival requires skill and courage undreamt of on other worlds. It is not surprising therefore that the men forming the Catachan Regiments are tough, resourceful and uncompromising warriors, deadly up close with their wicked knives or from ambush with their lasguns. In jungle terrain they are unsurpassed, with each Catachan being worth ten of any other regiment.

Preferred special weapon: Flamer
Preferred heavy weapon: Heavy Bolter

- Veterans
- Jungle Fighters
- Hardened Fighters
- Special Weapon squads
- Ogryn squads

Data ref: 687697+A

SAVLAR CHEM-DOGS

Scavengers and criminals from the dregs of Imperial society, the Savlar were pressed into service to fight in the Third War for Armageddon. Motivated by the right to keep what they looted and the threat of return to Savlar, they excelled in the cramped, noxious hive battlefields. In many ways the Savlar would only be tolerated in a war zone like Armageddon - much of their equipment is stolen from other Regiments and much of their courage comes from the use of nitro-chem inhalers.

Preferred special weapon: Flamer
Preferred heavy weapon: Heavy bolter

- Rough Rider squadrons
- Ogryn squads
- Special Equipment: Chem-inhalers
- Light Infantry
- Xeno-fighters: Orks

Data ref: 028534x48G

Success is commemorated. Failure merely remembered.

TERRAX GUARD

Terrax is the site of a major Schola Progenium facility, the Schola Excubitos. The Schola Progenium train many Imperial agents for war, notably Storm Troopers and Commissars, and their methods are rigorous and effective. The tithed regiments raised on Terrax have been trained under the auspices of the Scholae Excubitos and are truly moulded in its image almost as an entire regiment of Commissars.

Preferred special weapon: Meltagun
Preferred heavy weapon: Lascannon

- Independent Commissars
- Special Equipment: Carapace Armour
- Close Order Drill
- Grenadiers
- Storm Trooper squads

Data ref: 927P

A small mind is easily filled with faith

HARAKONI WARHAWKS

Harakon is a low gravity world with towering hives whose spires reach into the upper atmosphere. The Harakoni use grav-gliders to hunt Vapourwyrms in the mountain passes below, making them fearless of altitude and expert at judging air currents. These skills are put to good use by the Imperial Guard and many Warmasters owe their laurels to the courage of the Harakoni Warhawks.

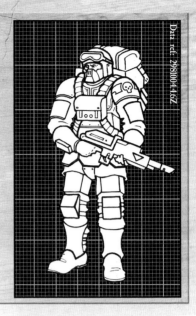

Preferred special weapon: Plasma Gun
Preferred heavy weapon: Heavy bolter

- Drop Troops
- Storm Trooper squads
- Special Equipment: Carapace Armour
- Heavy Weapon platoons
- Special Weapon squads

DEATH KORPS OF KRIEG

Krieg was laid to waste when rebellion led to a 500 year campaign of atomic purging. The Death Korps now seek to make amends for their earlier heresy by martyring themselves to the Imperial cause. The Death Korps fight without fear of death, disdaining retreat and surrender. They excel in grinding their enemies down in battles of attrition, making extensive use of razorwire and entrenchment.

Preferred special weapon: Meltagun
Preferred heavy weapon: Heavy bolter

- Rough Rider squadrons
- Iron Discipline
- Die-hards
- Hardened Fighters
- Storm Trooper squads
- Heavy Weapon platoons

KANAK SKULL TAKERS

The volcano-wracked world of Kanak is home to many fierce barbarian tribes, some of which are closer to Ogryn than human. Their talent for slaughter soon found a home in the Imperial Guard, where considerable tolerance for the feral tactics of the Kanak has been displayed. Like many feral regiments, service in the Imperial Guard is intended to teach them Imperial ways so that if they ever return to their homeworld they will be a civilising influence.

Preferred special weapon: Flamer
Preferred heavy weapon: rarely used

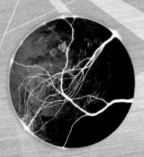

- Special Equipment: Warrior Weapons
- Ogryn squads
- Hardened Fighters
- Rough Riders squadrons
- Die-hards

Thought for the day: The end justifies the means.

IMPERIAL GUARD TERMS

Amasec – a widely available and highly alcoholic beverage distilled from wine.

Aquila/Sign of the Aquila – a sign of devotion to the Imperium that forms the Imperial Eagle, by crossing the hands with the palms pressed to chest and thumbs linked.

Augmetic – cybernetic/bionic, usually in the sense of body implants or repairs.

Bleed out – to die of blood loss before medical attention can be given.

Blunt – sanctioned psyker slang for a non-telepath.

Bone 'ead – an Ogryn sergeant with surgically augmented intelligence who can interpret orders for his less advanced squadmates. Also used as a term of abuse for anyone given to taking orders too literally to the detriment of their subordinates.

Catachan Kiss – headbutt.

Chart table/Chart desk – small, portable easel-like device for displaying tactical hololithic maps and three-dimensional terrain models. A chart desk is a heavier and usually non-portable version.

Codifier/cogitator/logic-engine – device empowered by the Machine Spirit to perform complex calculations and battlefield metriculations.

Cooker – meltagun.

Counterseptic – antiseptic and analgesic fluid used to combat infection.

Dataslate – hand-held device used to store and transfer information, imagery and orders.

Det-tape – tape peeled off to detonate tube-charges (time delay determined by length tape is trimmed to). Also used as general-purpose detonator material.

Do a Yarrick – to take a trophy from a slain enemy.

Emperor's Benediction – euphemism for mercy killing.

Enginseer – a Techpriest of the Adeptus Mechanicus charged with the responsibility for tending the machine spirits of a regiment's vehicles.

Flakboard – general purpose sheet material for defence and repair. Fitted to the inside walls of defensive positions to prevent spalling material – dislodged by weapon impacts – causing injury.

Found Wanting – euphemism for field execution by Commissar: "He was found wanting at the front line."

Freak, Brain, Bolt Magnet – derogatory terms for sanctioned psyker.

Fyceline – principal chemical ingredient used in the manufacture of standard Imperial Guard explosives.

Greenskin or 'Skin – Ork.

Gun-baby – whiteshield, conscript.

Hangman, Leash – derogatory terms for Commissar.

Hololithic – three-dimensional imagery.

Imperial Infantryman's Uplifting Primer – standard text manual issued to every Guardsman, containing proper procedure for everything from marching to bayonetting techniques. Also includes prescribed prayers and hymnals.

Interior Guard – general term, a world's PDF, or a Guard regiment given colonial duties.

Juvenat – as in 'juvenat processes' or 'juvenat drugs'. Techniques of prolonging youth and vitality. Usually highly expensive and reserved for senior officers or Imperial nobility.

Lamp-pack – standard Guard issue, compact lamp with internal (limited) power supply, designed to be hand held, or fix onto lasgun bayonet lugs.

Leftovers – an incomplete squad built from the remnants of squads that have suffered casualties.

Lho sticks – an addictive narcotic rolled into a compact tube and smoked by Guardsmen. Officio Medicae personnel have warned that they may cause respiratory illnesses and lung damage.

Long las – any model lasgun modified or designed for sniper use (as the name implies, they are usually longer than standard pattern weapons).

Magnoculars – powerful optical device for the magnification of distant objects. Can be modified to varying levels of complexity, with range finders, azimuth metriculators and heat-sensing equipment.

Micro-bead – (also micro-bead link, micro-bead intercom) small, short range vox system for inter-trooper communications in the field. Usually a small ear-plug with a tiny wire mouth-stalk. Generally only found on regiments from civilised or industrial worlds.

Multikey – universal key/lock pick.

Nine-seventies – Imperial Guard issue entrenching tool.

Obscura – prohibited narcotic.

One-way ticket – assignation to a grav-chute landing; "to be given a one-way ticket".

Pict – a video feed equivalent of vox.

Plank – idiot, also a derogatory term for Ogryn.

Promethium – A general term for fuel, but commonly used to refer to the highly volatile and incendiary jelly used as fuel in flamer units. Designed to adhere to the target and rapidly immolate them, promethium reaches extremely high temperatures within seconds of ignition and even continues to burn underwater.

Resuscitrex – Officio Medicae device incorporating a number of specialised devices, most frequently used to fibrillate patients who have suffered cardiac arrest.

Savlar – thief or drug addict.

Scope – general term for powered spotter sights; may be the telescopic sights on a long las, or a hand-held 'telescope' used by an officer.

Scrambled – insane, shell-shocked.

Screamer-Killer – Tyranid 'Carnifex' genus.

Shell – carapace armour.

Slap – disciplined by a senior officer for minor infraction (possession of unauthorised publications, for instance).

Spook – Tyranid 'Lictor' genus.

Sweeper/sweeper set/sweeper broom – man-portable mine detector.

The Emperor Protects – common soldier's blessing or refrain.

The Green (*Catachan*) – jungle terrain, Death world class jungle.

Torch – flamer.

Toy Soldiers, Glory Boys – Storm Troopers.

Tread Fether (*Tanith*) – man-portable, shoulder launched anti-tank weapon.

Tube-charges – 20cm (approx) long metal tubes filled with explosives for demolition work or grenades-type use.

Twist – Imperial slang for a mutant.

Vox-caster – a powerful, usually backpack-carried, communications gear. A 'vox set'.

Vox officer – the member of a squad or platoon trained to carry the vox-caster and operate it and other communications systems. General term for this branch of specialisation is 'Signals'.

IMPERIAL GUARD SUMMARY

	WS	BS	S	T	W	I	A	Ld	Sv
Heroic Senior Officer	4	4	3	3	3	4	3	9	5+
Senior Officer	4	4	3	3	2	4	3	8	5+
Junior Officer	4	4	3	3	1	3	2	8	5+
Platoon Commander	3	3	3	3	1	3	2	8	5+
Veteran Sergeant	3	3	3	3	1	3	2	8	5+
Guardsman	3	3	3	3	1	3	1	7	5+
Conscript	2	2	3	3	1	3	1	5	5+
Commissar	4	4	3	3	2	4	2	10	5+
Sanctioned Psyker	2	2	3	3	1	3	1	8	5+
Priest	4	4	3	3	2	4	2	8	-
Tech-Priest Enginseer	3	3	3	3	1	3	1	8	3+
Hardened Vet. Sgt.	3	4	3	3	1	3	2	8	5+
Hardened Veteran	3	4	3	3	1	3	1	8	5+
Storm Trooper Vet. Sgt.	3	4	3	3	1	3	2	8	4+
Storm Trooper	3	4	3	3	1	3	1	8	4+
Ogryn	4	3	5	4	3	3	2	8	5+
Ogryn Bone 'ead	4	3	5	4	3	3	3	9	5+
Ratling	2	4	2	2	1	4	1	6	5+

	WS	BS	S	Front	Side	Rear	I	A
Sentinel	3	3	5	10	10	10	3	1

	Front Armour	Side Armour	Rear Armour	BS
Basilisk	12	10	10	3
Chimera	12	10	10	3
Hellhound	13	12	10	3
Leman Russ	14	12	10	3
Demolisher	14	13	11	3

ORDNANCE WEAPONS	Range	Str.	AP	Type
Battle cannon	72"	8	3	Ordnance 1/Blast
Demolisher	24"	10	2	Ordnance 1/Blast
Earthshaker	120"	9	3	Ordnance 1/Blast

RANGED WEAPONS	Range	Str	AP	Type
Autocannon	48"	7	4	Heavy 2
Boltgun	24"	4	5	Rapid fire
Bolt pistol	12"	4	5	Pistol
Flamer	Template	4	5	Assault 1
Grenade launcher (frag)	24"	3	6	Assault 1 Blast*
Grenade launcher (krak)	24"	6	4	Assault 1*
Heavy bolter	36"	5	4	Heavy 3
Heavy flamer	Template	5	4	Assault 1
Heavy stubber	36"	4	6	Heavy 3
Hellpistol	12"	3	5	Pistol
Hellgun	24"	3	5	Rapid fire
Inferno cannon	24"	6	4	Heavy 1*
Lasgun	24"	3	–	Rapid fire
Laspistol	12"	3	–	Pistol
Lascannon	48"	9	2	Heavy 1
Meltagun	12"	8	1	Assault 1*
Missile launcher (frag)	48"	4	6	Heavy 1 Blast*
Missile launcher (krak)	48"	8	3	Heavy 1*
Mortar	G48"	4	6	Heavy 1 Blast
Multi-laser	36"	6	6	Heavy 3
Multi-melta	24"	8	1	Heavy 1*
Plasma cannon	36"	7	2	Heavy 1 Blast*
Plasma gun	24"	7	2	Rapid fire *
Plasma pistol	12"	7	2	Pistol*
Ripper gun	12"	4	6	Assault 2
Shotgun	12"	3	–	Assault 2
Sniper rifle	36"	X	6	Heavy 1*
Storm bolter	24"	4	5	Assault 2

These weapons have additional special rules. See the Weapons section in the Warhammer 40,000 rulebook or the relevant entry in this book for more details.

Five Doctrines may be bought from the following list. Full details and costs are to be found on pages 55-57

RESTRICTED TROOPS
One Doctrine must be used to allow use of each of the following units: Heavy Weapon Platoons, Priests, Storm Trooper Squads, Techpriest Enginseer, Ratling Squads, Sanctioned Psyker, Ogryn Squads, Special Weapon Squads, Conscript Platoons, Rough Rider Squadrons,

ALTERNATE ORGANISATION

DROP TROOPS
Any Guard Infantry unit (without a transport) or Sentinel Squadron may Deep Strike.

GRENADIERS
0-3 Storm Trooper squads may be included as Troops. These may not Deep Strike or infiltrate.

MECHANISED
All Guard Infantry units must take a Chimera transport whether they normally have the option or not.

SKILLS AND DRILLS.

CLOSE ORDER DRILL
+1 Leadership and +1 Initiative for units in close order.

DIE-HARDS
Units ignore negative morale modifiers for being outnumbered in close combat.

HARDENED FIGHTERS
Guard Infantry units gain +1 WS. Sentinels gain +1WS and +1 A.

INDEPENDENT COMMISSARS
1-3 Commissars, counting as independent characters, may be bought as an Elites choice, costing +10 points.

IRON DISCIPLINE
Unit using Ld of an Officer with Iron Discipline for a Morale or Pinning test ignores modifier for being under half strength and may regroup even if below half strength.

VETERANS
The normal 0-1 limit on Hardened Veteran units does not apply to this regiment.

JUNGLE FIGHTERS
- See 12" through forest or jungle terrain;
- 4+ cover save, move at full speed in wooded terrain;
- May infiltrate into wooded terrain'
- Infantry platoon squad may buy heavy flamer instead of heavy weapon.
- Jungle fighter units may never include lascannons.
- All units reduce armour save to 6+.

LIGHT INFANTRY
Guard Infantry without transport may:
- Roll additional dice for moving through difficult terrain.
- Infiltrate.
- Infantry platoon squad may buy sniper rifle instead of heavy weapon.

SHARPSHOOTERS
Guard Infantry model with BS of 3 may make a single re-roll of a shooting to hit roll of 1. The Sharpshooter ability has no effect on plasma weapons or sniper rifles.

XENOS-FIGHTERS
Against either Orks, Eldar (including Dark Eldar), or Tyranids, Guard Infantry unit or Sentinel squadron in close combat with enemy of that race hit on 3+. Does not apply if enemy is a Tyranid monstrous creature, monstrous creature or independent character.

SPECIAL EQUIPMENT
Each item uses up one Doctrine choice.

Chem-inhaler. Unit always tests morale, leadership or pinning with no negative modifiers. If they fail a morale test for 25% shooting casualties they will be pinned rather than falling back.

Cameleoline. +1 to all cover saves.

Carapace armour. 4+ Armour save.

Cyber-enhancement. 6+ Invulnerable save.

Warrior Weapons. Any model normally armed with a lasgun without access to the armoury replaces it with a laspistol and close combat weapon or a pair of close combat weapons.

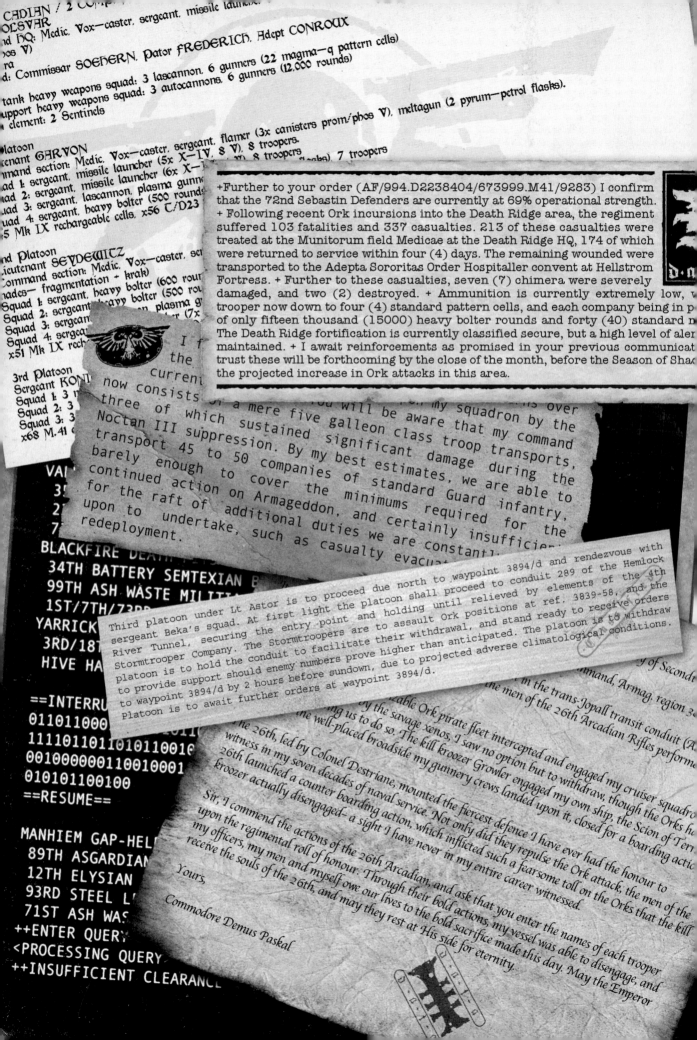

CADIAN / 2 COM...
...OLSVAR
...nd HQ: Medic, Vox—caster, sergeant, missile launch...
...os V)
...ra
...d: Commissar SOEHERN, Pator FREDERICH, Adept CONROUX

...tank heavy weapons squad: 3 lascannon, 6 gunners (22 magma—q pattern cells)
...upport heavy weapons squad: 3 autocannons, 6 gunners (12,000 rounds)
... element: 2 Sentinels

...latoon
...tenant GARVON
...mmand section: Medic, Vox—caster, sergeant, flamer (3x canisters prom/phos V), meltagun (2 pyrum—petrol flasks).
...ad 1: sergeant, missile launcher (5x X—IV, 8 V), 8 troopers.
...ad 2: sergeant, missile launcher (6x X—... 8 V), 8 troopers.
...ad 3: sergeant, lascannon, plasma gunn... ...asks) 7 troopers
...ad 4: sergeant, heavy bolter (500 rounds...
...5 Mk IX rechargeable cells, x56 C/D23...

...nd Platoon
...ieutenant SEYDEWITZ
...command section: Medic, Vox—caster, ser...
...nades— fragmentation + krak)
...Squad 1: sergeant, heavy bolter (600 rou...
...Squad 2: sergeant, heavy bolter (500 rou...
...Squad 3: sergeant, ...plasma g...
...Squad 4: sergeant, ...er (7x...
...x51 Mk IX rech...

3rd Platoon
Sergeant KON...
Squad 1: 3 m...
Squad 2: 3...
Squad 3: 3...
x68 M.41 c...

VA...
3...
2...
7...

BLACKFIRE DEA...
34TH BATTERY SEMTEXIAN B...
99TH ASH WASTE MILITI...
1ST/7TH/73R...
YARRICK...
3RD/18T...
HIVE HA...

==INTERRU...
011011000...
111101101101011001...
0010000001100100...
010101100100
==RESUME==

MANHIEM GAP-HELL...
89TH ASGARDIAN...
12TH ELYSIAN...
93RD STEEL L...
71ST ASH WAS...
++ENTER QUER...
<PROCESSING QUERY...
++INSUFFICIENT CLEARANCE...

+Further to your order (AF/994.D2238404/673999.M41/9283) I confirm that the 72nd Sebastin Defenders are currently at 69% operational strength. + Following recent Ork incursions into the Death Ridge area, the regiment suffered 103 fatalities and 337 casualties. 213 of these casualties were treated at the Munitorum field Medicae at the Death Ridge HQ, 174 of which were returned to service within four (4) days. The remaining wounded were transported to the Adepta Sororitas Order Hospitaller convent at Hellstrom Fortress. + Further to these casualties, seven (7) chimera were severely damaged, and two (2) destroyed. + Ammunition is currently extremely low, w... trooper now down to four (4) standard pattern cells, and each company being in p... of only fifteen thousand (15000) heavy bolter rounds and forty (40) standard n... The Death Ridge fortification is currently classified secure, but a high level of aler... maintained. + I await reinforcements as promised in your previous communicat... trust these will be forthcoming by the close of the month, before the Season of Shad... the projected increase in Ork attacks in this area.

...I f...
...the...
...current...
...now consists... ...of a mere five galleon class troop transports,
three of which sustained significant damage during the
Noctan III suppression. By my best estimates, we are able to
transport 45 to 50 companies of standard Guard infantry,
barely enough to cover the minimums required for the
continued action on Armageddon, and certainly insuffici...
for the raft of additional duties we are constantl...
upon to undertake, such as casualty evacu...
redeployment.

Third platoon under Lt Astor is to proceed due north to waypoint 3894/d and rendezvous with
sergeant Beka's squad. At first light the platoon shall proceed to conduit 289 of the Hemlock
River Tunnel, securing the entry point and holding until relieved by elements of the 4th
Stormtrooper Company. The Stormtroopers are to assault Ork positions at ref. 3839-58, and the
platoon is to hold the conduit to facilitate their withdrawal, and stand ready to receive orders
to provide support should enemy numbers prove higher than anticipated. The platoon is to withdraw
to waypoint 3894/d by 2 hours before sundown, due to projected adverse climatological conditions.
Platoon is to await further orders at waypoint 3894/d.

...able Ork pirate fleet intercepted and engaged my cruiser squadro...
... by the savage xenos, I saw no option but to withdraw, though the Orks ha...
...well-placed broadside my gunnery crews landed upon it, closed for a boarding actio...
...The 26th, led by Colonel Destriane, mounted the fiercest defence I have ever had the honour to
...witness in my seven decades of naval service. Not only did they repulse the Ork attack, the men of the
...26th launched a counter boarding action, which inflicted such a fearsome toll on the Orks that the kill
...kroozer actually disengaged– a sight I have never in my entire career witnessed.

...the trans-Jopall transit conduit (A...
...the men of the 26th Arcadian Rifles perform...
...nmand, Armag. region 3...
...y of Secondit...

Sir, I commend the actions of the 26th Arcadian, and ask that you enter the names of each trooper
upon the regimental roll of honour. Through their bold actions, my vessel was able to disengage, and
my officers, my men and myself owe our lives to the bold sacrifice made this day. May the Emperor
receive the souls of the 26th, and may they rest at His side for eternity.

Yours,

Commodore Demus Paskal